U·X·L
Encyclopedia
of Science

U·X·L
Encyclopedia
of Science

Second Edition
Volume 4: D-Em

Rob Nagel, Editor

U·X·L

GALE GROUP

THOMSON LEARNING

Detroit • New York • San Diego • San Francisco
Boston • New Haven, Conn. • Waterville, Maine
London • Munich

U·X·L
Encyclopedia of Science
Second Edition

Rob Nagel, *Editor*

Staff

Elizabeth Shaw Grunow, *U•X•L Editor*

Julie Carnagie, *Contributing Editor*

Carol DeKane Nagel, *U•X•L Managing Editor*

Thomas L. Romig, *U•X•L Publisher*

Shalice Shah-Caldwell, *Permissions Associate (Pictures)*

Robyn Young, *Imaging and Multimedia Content Editor*

Rita Wimberley, *Senior Buyer*

Pamela A. E. Galbreath, *Senior Art Designer*

Michelle Cadorée, *Indexing*

GGS Information Services, *Typesetting*

On the front cover: Nikola Tesla with one of his generators, reproduced by permission of the Granger Collection.

On the back cover: The flow of red blood cells through blood vessels, reproduced by permission of Phototake.

Library of Congress Cataloging-in-Publication Data

U-X-L encyclopedia of science.—2nd ed. / Rob Nagel, editor
  p.cm.
  Includes bibliographical references and indexes.
  Contents: v.1. A-As — v.2. At-Car — v.3. Cat-Cy — v.4. D-Em — v.5. En-G — v.6. H-Mar — v.7. Mas-O — v.8. P-Ra — v.9. Re-St — v.10. Su-Z.
  Summary: Includes 600 topics in the life, earth, and physical sciences as well as in engineering, technology, math, environmental science, and psychology.
  ISBN 0-7876-5432-9 (set : acid-free paper) — ISBN 0-7876-5433-7 (v.1 : acid-free paper) — ISBN 0-7876-5434-5 (v.2 : acid-free paper) — ISBN 0-7876-5435-3 (v.3 : acid-free paper) — ISBN 0-7876-5436-1 (v.4 : acid-free paper) — ISBN 0-7876-5437-X (v.5 : acid-free paper) — ISBN 0-7876-5438-8 (v.6 : acid-free paper) — ISBN 0-7876-5439-6 (v.7 : acid-free paper) — ISBN 0-7876-5440-X (v.8 : acid-free paper) — ISBN 0-7876-5441-8 (v.9 : acid-free paper) — ISBN 0-7876-5775-1 (v.10 : acid-free paper)
  1. Science-Encyclopedias, Juvenile. 2. Technology-Encyclopedias, Juvenile. [1. Science-Encyclopedias. 2. Technology-Encyclopedias.] I. Title: UXL encyclopedia of science. II. Nagel, Rob.
Q121.U18 2001
503-dc21
                                        2001035562

Printed in the United States of America

10 9 8 7 6 5 4 3 2 1

Table of Contents

Contents

Reader's Guide

Demystify scientific theories, controversies, discoveries, and phenomena with the *U•X•L Encyclopedia of Science,* Second Edition.

This alphabetically organized ten-volume set opens up the entire world of science in clear, nontechnical language. More than 600 entries—an increase of more than 10 percent from the first edition—provide fascinating facts covering the entire spectrum of science. This second edition features more than 50 new entries and more than 100 updated entries. These informative essays range from 250 to 2,500 words, many of which include helpful sidebar boxes that highlight fascinating facts and phenomena. Topics profiled are related to the physical, life, and earth sciences, as well as to math, psychology, engineering, technology, and the environment.

In addition to solid information, the *Encyclopedia* also provides these features:

- "Words to Know" boxes that define commonly used terms
- Extensive cross references that lead directly to related entries
- A table of contents by scientific field that organizes the entries
- More than 600 color and black-and-white photos and technical drawings
- Sources for further study, including books, magazines, and Web sites

Each volume concludes with a cumulative subject index, making it easy to locate quickly the theories, people, objects, and inventions discussed throughout the *U•X•L Encyclopedia of Science,* Second Edition.

Suggestions

We welcome any comments on this work and suggestions for entries to feature in future editions of *U•X•L Encyclopedia of Science.* Please write: Editors, *U•X•L Encyclopedia of Science,* U•X•L, Gale Group, 27500 Drake Road, Farmington Hills, Michigan, 48331-3535; call toll-free: 800-877-4253; fax to: 248-699-8097; or send an e-mail via www.galegroup.com.

Entries by Scientific Field

Astrophysics

Biology

Technology

Dam

Dams are structures that hold back water in a stream or river, forming a lake or reservoir behind the wall. Dams are used as flood control devices and as sources of hydroelectric power and water for crops. Dams are designed to resist the force of the water against them, the force of standing water—not a running stream.

Dam construction

There are five main types of dams: arch, buttress, earth, gravity, and rock-fill. Arch dams are curved upstream, into the water they hold back. They are typically built in narrow canyons, where the high rocky walls of the canyon can withstand the pressure of the water as it pushes off the arch and against the walls.

A buttress dam uses the force of the water to support it. A slab of concrete is tilted at a 45-degree angle and has buttresses (supports) on the opposite side of the water. While the water pushes down on the slab, the buttresses push up against it. These counterforces keep the slab in balance. Because of the large number of steel beams needed in construction, however, these dams are no longer popular because steel and labor are too expensive.

An earth dam may be a simple embankment or mound of earth (gravel, sand, clay) holding back water. An earth dam might also have a core of cement or a watertight material lining the upstream side.

A gravity dam, made of cement or masonry, withstands the force of the water behind it with its weight. To accomplish this, a gravity dam's base must have a width that is at least two-thirds the total height of the dam. The dam wall is typically given a slight curve, which adds extra strength and watertightness.

Rock-fill dams are embankments of loose rocks covering a watertight core, such as clay. The upstream side of a rock-fill dam might also be constructed with a watertight material.

Impact of dams

While dams can help save lives, irrigate farmland, and provide hydroelectric power, they can also damage farmland and the environment.

A downstream view of Hoover Dam, looking toward the east at the face of the dam. The Colorado River is in the foreground. The dam is 726 feet (221 meters) high and confines enough water in Lake Mead to cover the state of New York one foot deep. *(Reproduced by permission of The Stock Market.)*

Building a dam changes the ecology of the surrounding area, flooding the habitats of plants and animals. Currently, before a dam is built a full-scale environmental impact study is made to determine if any endangered species would be threatened by a dam's construction.

In some areas of the world, however, progress far outweighs the need to protect endangered species or the lives of many people. This seems to be the case, with the giant Three Gorges Dam being built on the Yangtze River in central China. Expected to be completed sometime in 2003, the dam will create the world's largest hydroelectric project and a huge new lake. It will stretch nearly 1 mile (1.6 kilometers) across and tower 575 feet (175 meters) above the world's third-longest river. Its reservoir would stretch more than 350 miles (563 kilometers) upstream. By the time the newly created reservoir reaches its maximum height in 2008, it is estimated that 1.1 million people will have been relocated (some sources say as many as 1.9 million people). Many international organizations have criticized the project, saying it threatens the environment and dislocates many people who are merely being resettled in already over-crowded areas.

Dark matter

Dark matter is the term astronomers use to describe material in the universe that does not emit or reflect light and is, therefore, invisible. Stars, nebulae, and galaxies are examples of luminous objects in the sky. However, luminous matter appears to make up only a small fraction of all the matter in the universe, perhaps only up to 10 percent. The rest of the matter is cold and dark, hidden from people's direct view.

The principal way dark matter can be detected is by observing its gravitational effect on nearby objects. Although dark matter does not shine, it still exerts a gravitational force on the matter around it. Astronomers believe that dark matter is a "cosmic glue" holding together rapidly spinning galaxies and controlling the rate at which the universe expands.

How can we know what we cannot see?

Understanding something that cannot be seen is difficult, but it is not impossible. Present-day astronomers study dark matter by its effects on the bright matter that can be observed. It was in the 1930s that Swiss astronomer Fritz Zwicky first pointed out that dark matter must exist.

Words to Know

Black dwarf: Remains of a white dwarf star that has stopped glowing.

Black hole: Single point of infinite mass and gravity formed when a massive star burns out its nuclear fuel and collapses under its own gravitational force.

Brown dwarf: Blob of celestial gas not massive and hot enough to trigger the nuclear reaction at its core that would classify it as a star.

Subatomic particle: Basic unit of matter and energy smaller than an atom.

White dwarf: Dense, faintly glowing core left when a medium-sized star stops burning.

Zwicky claimed that the mass of known matter in galaxies is not great enough to generate the gravitational force to hold a cluster of galaxies together. Each independent galaxy moves at too great a speed for galaxies to remain in a cluster. Yet the galaxies were not spinning away from each other. They had to be held together by a gravitational field created by undetected mass.

More than 40 years later, American astronomer Vera Rubin found that the same principle is true within a single galaxy. The mass of stars alone do not exert enough gravitational pull to hold the galaxy together. She discovered that stars in the far reaches of the galaxy rotate about the galactic center at the same speed as stars close to the center. Rubin concluded that some invisible, massive substance surrounds a galaxy, exerting gravitational force on all its stars.

Sources of dark matter?

Astronomers have only been able to speculate on the composition of dark matter. One source of dark matter might be the diffuse, dark "halo" of gas in and around galaxies that increases their mass. Another might be dark objects called MACHOs (MAssive Compact Halo Objects) that lurk invisibly in the halos surrounding galaxies and galactic clusters. MACHOs are planets or stars made up of ordinary matter that are too faint to be observed directly. However, they can act as a gravitational lens and magnify the brightness of brighter stars behind them.

Astronomers have also considered that dark matter may be super-massive black holes (single points of infinite mass and gravity formed from the collapse of burned-out massive stars) at the centers of galaxies. These black holes may be contributing several hundred million or even a billion solar masses to the galaxies in which they reside. One more possible source of dark matter could be multitudes of WIMPs (Weakly Interacting Massive Particles), exotic, unfamiliar particles that may exist all around us. Astronomers have theorized about the existence of these particles, although experiments have not yet confirmed their presence.

A composite image of a cluster of galaxies and the gas cloud in which they are embedded. The cloud is considered to be evidence for the existence of dark matter because the gravitational pull of the cluster alone is not strong enough to hold it together. Some astronomers have suggested that it is dark matter that is preventing the cloud from dispersing into space. *(Reproduced by permission of National Aeronautics and Space Administration.)*

The search for the truth about dark matter is inextricably tied in with other outstanding questions in cosmology: How much mass does the universe contain? How did galaxies form? Will the universe expand forever? Dark matter is so important to the understanding of the size, shape, and ultimate fate of the universe that the search for it will very likely dominate astronomy until an answer is found.

Dating techniques

Dating techniques are procedures used by scientists to determine the age of an object or a series of events. The two main types of dating methods are relative and absolute. Relative dating methods are used to determine only if one sample is older or younger than another. Absolute dating methods are used to determine an actual date in years for the age of an object.

Relative dating

Before the advent of absolute dating methods in the twentieth century, nearly all dating was relative. The main relative dating method is stratigraphy (pronounced stra-TI-gra-fee), which is the study of layers of rocks or the objects embedded within those layers. This method is based on the assumption (which nearly always holds true) that deeper layers of rock were deposited earlier in Earth's history, and thus are older than more shallow layers. The successive layers of rock represent successive intervals of time.

Since certain species of animals existed on Earth at specific times in history, the fossils or remains of such animals embedded within those successive layers of rock also help scientists determine the age of the layers. Similarly, pollen grains released by seed-bearing plants became fossilized in rock layers. If a certain kind of pollen is found in an archaeological site, scientists can check when the plant that produced that pollen lived to determine the relative age of the site.

Absolute dating

Absolute dating methods are carried out in a laboratory. Absolute dates must agree with dates from other relative methods in order to be valid. The most widely used and accepted form of absolute dating is radioactive decay dating.

Radioactive decay dating. Radioactive decay refers to the process in which a radioactive form of an element is converted into a nonra-

▼ Words to Know

Cosmic rays: Invisible, high-energy particles that constantly bombard Earth from all directions in space.

Dendrochronology: Also known as tree-ring dating, the science concerned with determining the age of trees by examining their growth rings.

Half-life: Measurement of the time it takes for one-half of a radioactive substance to decay.

Radioactive decay: The predictable manner in which a population of atoms of a radioactive element spontaneously disintegrate over time.

Stratigraphy: Study of layers of rocks or the objects embedded within those layers.

dioactive product at a regular rate. The nucleus of every radioactive element (such as radium and uranium) spontaneously disintegrates over time, transforming itself into the nucleus of an atom of a different element. In the process of disintegration, the atom gives off radiation (energy emitted in the form of waves). Hence the term radioactive decay. Each element decays at its own rate, unaffected by external physical conditions. By measuring the amount of original and transformed atoms in an object, scientists can determine the age of that object.

The age of the remains of plants, animals, and other organic material can be determined by measuring the amount of carbon-14 contained in that material. Carbon-14, a radioactive form of the element carbon, is created in the atmosphere by cosmic rays (invisible, high-energy particles that constantly bombard Earth from all directions in space). When carbon-14 falls to Earth, it is absorbed by plants. These plants are eaten by animals who, in turn, are eaten by even larger animals. Eventually, the entire ecosystem (community of plants and animals) of the planet, including humans, is filled with a concentration of carbon-14. As long as an organism is alive, the supply of carbon-14 is replenished. When the organism dies, the supply stops, and the carbon-14 contained in the organism begins to spontaneously decay into nitrogen-14. The time it takes for one-half of the carbon-14 to decay (a period called a half-life) is 5,730 years. By measuring the amount of carbon-14 remaining, scientists can pinpoint the exact date of the organism's death. The range of conventional radiocarbon dating is 30,000 to 40,000 years. With sensitive instrumentation, this range can be extended to 70,000 years.

In addition to the radiocarbon dating technique, scientists have developed other dating methods based on the transformation of one element into another. These include the uranium-thorium method, the potassium-argon method, and the rubidium-strontium method.

Thermoluminescence. Thermoluminescence (pronounced ther-moe-loo-mi-NES-ence) dating is very useful for determining the age of pot-

Dendrochronology is a dating technique that makes use of tree growth rings. *(Reproduced by permission of The Stock Market.)*

tery. When a piece of pottery is heated in a laboratory at temperatures more than 930°F (500°C), electrons from quartz and other minerals in the pottery clay emit light. The older the pottery, the brighter the light that will be emitted. Using thermoluminescence, pottery pieces as old as 100,000 years can be dated with precision.

Tree-ring dating. Known as dendrochronology (pronounced den-dro-crow-NOL-o-gee), tree-ring dating is based on the fact that trees produce one growth ring each year. Narrow rings grow in cold or dry years, and wide rings grow in warm or wet years. The rings form a distinctive pattern, which is the same for all members in a given species and geographical area. Thus, the growth pattern of a tree of a known age can be used as a standard to determine the age of similar trees. The ages of buildings and archaeological sites can also be determined by examining the ring patterns of the trees used in their construction. Dendrochronology has a range of 1 to 10,000 years or more.

DDT (dichlorodiphenyl-trichloroethane)

DDT is a synthetic chemical compound once used widely in the United States and throughout the world as a pesticide (a chemical substance used to kill weeds, insects, rodents, or other pests). It is probably best known for its dual nature: although remarkably effective in destroying certain living things that are harmful to plants and animals, it can also be extremely dangerous to humans and the environment.

The abbreviation DDT stands for dichlorodiphenyltrichloroethane. DDT was first produced in the laboratory in 1873. For more than half a century, it was little more than a laboratory curiosity—a complicated synthetic (produced by scientists) compound with no apparent use.

Then, in 1939, Swiss chemist Paul Hermann Müller (1899–1965) discovered that DDT was highly poisonous to insects. The discovery was very important because of its potential for use in killing insects that cause disease and eat agricultural crops. For his work, Müller was awarded the Nobel Prize in medicine in 1948.

DDT as an insecticide

During and after World War II (1939–45), DDT became extremely popular among public health workers, farmers, and foresters. Peak production of the compound reached 386 million pounds (175 million kilograms) globally in 1970. Between 1950 and 1970, 22,204 tons (20,000 metric tons) of DDT was used annually in the former Soviet Union. The greatest use of DDT in the United States occurred in 1959, when 79 million pounds (36 million kilograms) of the chemical were sprayed.

By the early 1970s, however, serious questions were being raised about the environmental effects of DDT. Reports indicated that harmless insects (such as bees), fish, birds, and other animals were being killed or harmed as a result of exposure to DDT. The pesticide was even blamed for the near-extinction of at least one bird, the peregrine falcon. Convinced that the environmental damage from DDT was greater than the compound's possible benefits, the U.S. Environmental Protection Agency banned the use of DDT in the United States in 1973. Its use in certain other countries has continued, however, since some nations face health and environmental problems quite different from those of the United States.

DDT's environmental problems arise because of two important properties: persistence and lipid-solubility. The term persistence refers to the fact that DDT does not break down very easily. Once the pesticide has been used in an area, it is likely to remain there for many years. In addition, DDT does not dissolve in water, although it does dissolve in fatty or oily liquids. (The term lipid-solubility is used because fats and oils are

Before the dangers of DDT were known, crops and people alike were sprayed with the chemical to protect against bothersome insects. *(Reproduced courtesy of the Library of Congress.)*

members of the organic family known as lipids.) Since DDT is not soluble in water, it is not washed away by the rain, adding to its persistence in the environment. But since DDT *is* lipid-soluble, it tends to concentrate in the body fat of animals. The following sequence of events shows how DDT can become a problem for many animals in a food web.

DDT is used today in such African nations as Zimbabwe and Ethiopia to control mosquitoes and the tsetse fly. These two insects cause serious diseases, such as malaria and sleeping sickness. DDT saves lives when used on the tsetse fly in Lake Kariba in Zimbabwe. But once sprayed on

Clutch of mallard eggs contaminated by DDT. The accumulation of DDT in many birds causes reproductive difficulties. Eggs have thinner shells that break easily, and some eggs may not hatch at all. *(Reproduced by permisson of the National Geographic Image Collection.)*

the lake, DDT does not disappear very quickly. Instead, it is taken up by plants and animals that live in the lake. Studies have shown that the concentration of DDT in the lake itself is only 0.002 parts per billion. But algae in the lake have a concentration of 2.5 parts per million. Other members of the food web also accumulate DDT from the organisms they eat. Fish that feed on the algae have DDT levels of 2 parts per million; tiger-fish and cormorants (both of whom live on the algae-eating fish) have levels of 5 and 10 parts per million, respectively; and crocodiles (who eat both tiger-fish and cormorants) have levels as high as 34 parts per million.

Bans on the use of DDT in the United States and some other nations have given ecosystems in those countries a chance to recover. Populations of peregrine falcons, for example, have begun to stabilize and grow once again. Many other animal species are no longer at risk from DDT. Of course, poor nations continue to face a more difficult choice than does the United States, since they must balance the protection of the health of their human populations against the protection of their natural ecosystems.

In December 2000, in a convention organized by the United Nations Environment Program, 122 nations agreed to a treaty banning twelve very toxic chemicals. Included among the twelve was DDT. However, the treaty allowed the use of DDT to combat malaria until other alternatives become available. Before it can take effect, the treaty must be ratified by 50 of the nations that agreed to it in principle.

Dementia

Dementia is a decline in a person's ability to think and learn. It is an irreversible mental condition. Occurring mainly in older people, dementia is characterized by memory loss, the inability to concentrate and make judgments, and the general loss of other intellectual abilities.

The two most common forms of dementia are senile dementia and Alzheimer's disease. Senile dementia, or senility, is the loss of mental capacities as a result of old age. It is considered a normal part of the aging process, and generally occurs very late in life. Alzheimer's disease, on the other hand, is not a normal result of aging and can begin in late middle age.

The deterioration of brain tissue occurs much more quickly in those people suffering from Alzheimer's disease than in those suffering from senility. Alzheimer's disease is marked first by forgetfulness, followed by memory loss and disorientation, then by severe memory loss, confusion,

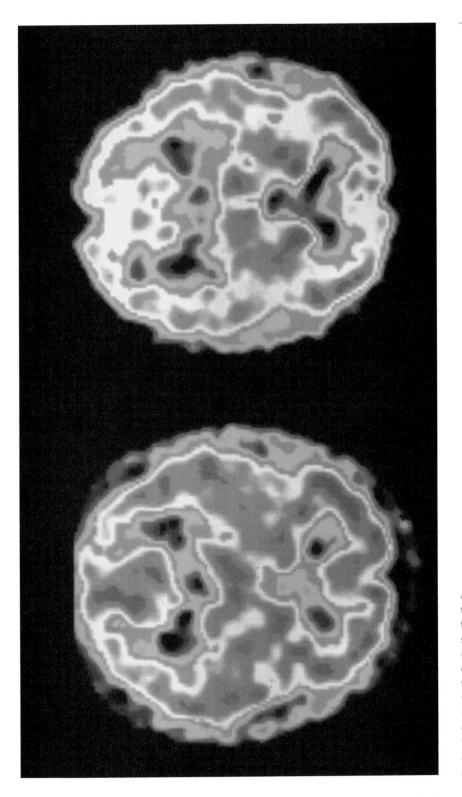

A colored positron emission tomography (PET) scan of the brain of an AIDS patient suffering from dementia (top). Compared to the scan of a normal brain (bottom), the dark areas of the brain in the AIDS patient are much smaller, reflecting a decrease in the brain's ability to function. *(Reproduced by permission of Photo Researchers, Inc.)*

and delusions. There is no effective treatment or cure for the disease and its cause is unknown.

Dementia may result from several other conditions characterized by progressive deterioration of the brain. The three most common of these are Pick's disease, Parkinson's disease, and Huntington's disease.

Like Alzheimer's disease, Pick's disease affects the brain's cortex—the outer part where most of the higher mental functions take place. However, Pick's disease affects different parts of the cortex than does Alzheimer's disease. This influences the order in which symptoms appear. The earliest symptoms of Pick's disease include personality changes such as loss of tact (politeness) and concern for others. Loss of language skills occurs afterward, while memory and knowledge of such things as where one is and the time of day are preserved until much later.

Both Parkinson's disease and Huntington's disease initially affect deeper brain structures, those that control muscular movements. Symptoms of Parkinson's disease, which begins in middle to later life, include trembling of the lips and hands, loss of facial expression, and muscular rigidity. In later stages, about 50 percent of patients with the disease develop some degree of dementia. Huntington's disease, which strikes in middle age, is first marked by involuntary muscular movements. Shortly after, patients suffering from the disease begin to have trouble thinking clearly and remembering previous events. In later stages of the illness, Huntington patients cannot walk or care for themselves.

[*See also* **Alzheimer's disease; Nervous system**]

Density

Density is defined as the mass of a unit volume of some material. The term unit volume means the amount contained in one volumetric unit of measurement: one cubic foot, one liter, or one milliliter, for example. The density of pure iron, for instance, is 7.87 grams per cubic centimeter (7.87 g/cm^3). That statement means that one cubic centimeter (1 cm^3) of iron has a mass of 7.87 grams.

Density is an important measurement because it allows for the comparison of the heaviness of two materials. Rather than asking, "Which is heavier: iron or Styrofoam^{TM}?," the proper question to ask is: "Which is more dense: iron or Styrofoam^{TM}?" This question is more appropriate because it asks about a comparison between equal amounts of two different materials.

Specific gravity

Another form of measurement closely associated with density is specific gravity. The specific gravity of a material is the density of that material compared to the density of some standard. For solids and liquids, the most common standard is water, whose density is 1.00 gram per cubic centimeter. The specific gravity of iron, then, is its density (7.87 grams per cubic centimeter) divided by the density of water (1.00 gram per cubic centimeter). You can see that the numerical value for the specific gravity of a solid or liquid is always the same as that of its density.

The oil in this beaker is layered on top of the water because it is less dense than the water. Similarly, the cork floats on the oil because it is less dense than either the oil or the water. *(Reproduced by permission of Phototake.)*

The reason is that the divisor in every case is 1 gram per cubic centimeter, the density of water. For iron, the specific gravity is 7.87. The only difference between density and specific gravity for solids and liquids is that specific gravity has no label. In dividing 7.87 grams per cubic centimeter by 1.00 gram per cubic centimeter, the labels divide out (cancel), leaving only the number.

The specific gravity of gases is somewhat more difficult since the most common standards are air (density = 1.293 grams per cubic centimeter) or hydrogen (density = 0.0899 gram per cubic centimeter). The specific gravity of oxygen using air as a standard, then, is its density (1.429 grams per cubic centimeter) divided by the density of air (1.293 grams per cubic centimeter), or 1.105. Using hydrogen as a standard, the specific gravity of oxygen is 1.429 grams per cubic centimeter ÷ 0.0899 gram per cubic centimeter, or 15.9.

Dentistry

Dentistry is the medical field concerned with the treatment and care of the teeth, the gums, and the oral cavity. This includes treating teeth damaged by tooth decay, accidents, or disease. Dentistry is considered an independent medical art, with its own licensing procedure. Orthodontics is the branch of dentistry concerned with tooth problems such as gaps between the teeth, crowded teeth, and irregular bite. Periodontics, another branch, focuses on gum problems.

Historical dental practices

Dental disease has been one of the most common ailments known to humankind. Ancient men and women worked hard to alleviate dental pain. As early as 1550 B.C., Egyptians used various remedies for toothache, which included such familiar ingredients as dough, honey, onions, incense, and fennel seeds.

The Egyptians also turned to superstition for help in preventing tooth pain. The mouse, which was considered to be protected by the Sun and capable of fending off death, was often used by individuals with a toothache. A common remedy involved applying half of the body of a dead mouse to the aching tooth while the body was still warm.

The Greek physician Hippocrates (c. 460–c. 377 B.C.), considered the father of medicine, believed that food lodged between teeth was responsible for tooth decay. He suggested pulling teeth that were loose and

Words to Know

Amalgam: Mixture of mercury and other metal elements used in making tooth cements.

Bridge: Partial denture anchored to adjacent teeth.

Denture: Set of false teeth.

Gingivitis: Gum inflammation.

Orthodontics: Branch of dentistry concerned with tooth problems such as gaps between the teeth, crowded teeth, and irregular bite.

Periodontics: Branch of dentistry focusing on gum problems.

Periodontitis: Gum disease involving damage to the periodontal ligament, which connects each tooth to the bone.

Plaque: Deposit of bacteria and their products on the surface of teeth.

decayed. Hippocrates also offered advice for bad breath. He suggested a mouth wash containing oil of anise seed, myrrh, and white wine.

Clean teeth were valued by the ancient Romans. Rich families had slaves clean their mouths using small sticks of wood and tooth powder. Such powders could include burned eggshell, bay leaves, and myrrh. These powders could also include more unusual ingredients, such as burned heads of mice and lizard livers. Earthworms marinated in vinegar were used for a mouth wash, and urine was thought of as a gum strengthener.

The Chinese were the first to develop an amalgam (mixture of metals) filling, which was mentioned in medical texts as early as 659. The Chinese also developed full dentures by the twelfth century and invented the toothbrush model for our contemporary toothbrushes in the fifteenth century.

The writings of Abu al-Qasim (936–1013), a Spanish Arab surgeon, influenced Islamic and European medical practitioners. He described surgery for dental irregularities, the use of gold wire to make teeth more stable, and the use of artificial teeth made of ox-bone. Abu al-Qasim (also known as Abulcasis) was one of the first to document the size and shape of dental tools, including drawings of dental saws, files, and extraction forceps.

The father of modern dentistry is considered to be French dentist Pierre Fauchard (1678–1761). Fauchard's work included filling teeth with lead or gold leaf tin foil. He also made various types of dentures and crowns from ivory or human teeth. In his influential writings, Fauchard explained how to straighten teeth and how to protect teeth against periodontal damage. Fauchard also took aim at some of the dental superstitions of the day, which included the mistaken belief that worms in the mouth played a role in tooth decay.

The development of many dental tools and practices in the nineteenth century laid the groundwork for present-day dentistry. Many of the great advances were made by Americans. The world's first dental school, the Baltimore College of Dentistry, opened in 1847. Around this time, anesthesia such as ether and nitrous oxide (laughing gas) was first used by dentists on patients having their teeth pulled. The practice of dentistry was further changed by the development of a drill powered by a foot pedal in 1871 and powered by electricity in 1872.

Another major discovery of the era was the X ray by German physicist Wilhelm Conrad Röntgen (1845–1923) in 1895. The first X ray of the teeth was made in 1896. Contemporary dentists continue to use X rays extensively to determine the condition of the teeth and the roots.

Cavities and fillings

Dental cavities, or caries, are perhaps the most common type of present-day oral disease. Cavities occur when bacteria forms a dental plaque on the surface of the tooth. Plaque, which is sticky and colorless, is a deposit of bacteria and their products. After the plaque is formed, food and the bacteria combine to create acids that slowly dissolve the substance of the tooth. The result is a hole in the tooth that must be filled or greater damage may occur, including eventual loss of the tooth.

The process of fixing dental cavities can be a short procedure depending on the size of the cavity. Small cavities may require no anesthesia and minimal drilling. Extensive dental cavities may require extensive drilling and novocaine or nitrous oxide to dull the pain. The process of

Teeth damaged by dental cavities can be excavated and filled with amalgam. *(Reproduced by permission of The Gale Group.)*

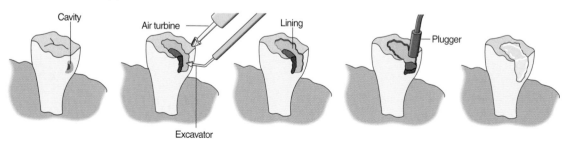

filling a cavity typically begins with the dentist using a drill or a hand tool to grind down the part of the tooth surrounding the cavity. The dentist then shapes the cavity, removes debris from the cavity, and dries it off. A cement lining is then added to insulate the inside of the tooth. The cavity is filled by inserting an amalgam or some other substance in small increments, compressing the material soundly.

Teeth are usually filled with an amalgam including silver, copper, tin, mercury, indium, and palladium. Other materials may be used for front teeth where metallic fillings would stand out. These include plastic composite material, which can be made to match tooth color.

Tooth replacement

Teeth that have large cavities, are badly discolored, or badly broken are often capped with a crown, which covers all or part of the damaged tooth. A crown can be made of gold or dental porcelain. Dental cement is used to keep the crown in place.

Bridges are devices that clasp new teeth in place, keep decayed teeth strong, and support the teeth in a proper arrangement. Some are removable by the dentist, and may be attached to the mouth by screws or soft cement. Others, called fixed bridges, are intended to be permanent.

A dentist examining a patient's teeth using digital subtraction radiography, a computerized X-ray technique. This new technology reveals details of the teeth and surrounding gum and bone tissue that traditional X rays cannot detect. *(Reproduced by permission of Photo Researchers, Inc.)*

Dentures, a set of replacement teeth, are used when all or a large part of the teeth must be replaced. New teeth can be made of acrylic resin or porcelain. A base in which to set the teeth must be designed to fit the mouth exactly. An impression of the existing teeth and jaws is taken to form this base. Modern dentists generally use acrylic plastics as the base for dentures. Acrylic plastic is mixed as a dough, heated, molded, and set in shape.

Gum disease

Gum disease is an immense problem among adults. Common gum diseases include gingivitis and periodontitis. Gingivitis is the inflammation of gum tissue, and is marked by bleeding, swollen gums. Periodontitis involves damage to the periodontal ligament, which connects each tooth to the bone. It also involves damage to the alveolar bone to which teeth are attached.

Periodontitis and gingivitis are caused primarily by bacterial dental plaque. This plaque includes bacteria that produces destructive enzymes in the mouth. These enzymes can damage cells and connective tissue. Untreated periodontal disease results in exposure of tooth root surfaces and pockets between the teeth and supporting tissue. This leaves teeth and roots open to decay, ending in tooth loss. When damage from the disease is too great, periodontal surgery is performed to clean out and regenerate the damaged area.

The art of moving teeth

The position of teeth in the mouth can be shaped and changed gradually using pressure. To straighten teeth, dentists usually apply braces. Braces are made up of a network of wires and bands of stainless steel or clear plastic. The bands are often anchored on the molars at the back of the mouth and the wires are adjusted to provide steady pressure on the surface of the teeth. This pressure slowly moves the teeth to a more desirable location in the mouth and enables new bone to build up where it is needed. Braces are usually applied to patients in their early teens and are worn for a specific period of time.

Depression

Depression is one of the most common mood disorders. Everyone experiences depressed moods from time to time. More commonly referred to

Words to Know

Bipolar disorder: Formerly manic-depressive illness, a condition in which a patient exhibits both an excited state called mania and a depressed state.

Electroconvulsive therapy: A form of treatment for depression in which an electric current is passed through the brain to produce convulsions.

Lithium: Natural mineral salt used as a medication to treat bipolar disorder.

Mania: Condition in which a person experiences exaggerated levels of elation.

Neurotransmitter: Chemical that transmits electrical impulses from one cell in the nervous system to another.

as "having the blues" or "being down in the dumps," the sad or depressed mood usually lasts for only a short period. When the feeling persists for weeks without apparent reason, however, it may be a sign of major depression, a psychiatric disorder.

The symptoms of major depression include a sad or depressed mood or a marked lack of interest and pleasure in almost all activities. This feeling persists for most of the day, nearly every day, for at least two weeks. In addition, many or all of the following symptoms occur: (1) loss of appetite; (2) fatigue (tiredness); (3) difficulty sleeping; (4) feelings of guilt or worthlessness; (5) lack of concentration; (6) thoughts of death, often including suicidal thoughts or plans, or even a suicide attempt.

People with major depression are also very likely to experience headaches, stomachaches, or pains or aches almost anywhere in their bodies. Major depression affects twice as many women during their lifetimes as it does men.

Causes of depression

No one knows the fundamental cause of major depression. Scientists believe this disorder might be caused by a low level of certain chemicals in the body known as neurotransmitters (pronounced nur-o-trans-

MI-ter). These are chemicals that transmit information (electrical impulses) from one cell in the nervous system to another.

Thus, depression may be more a biological than a psychological disorder. This conclusion is supported by the way depression often runs in families: up to 25 percent of those with depression have a relative with a mood disorder of some kind. Furthermore, if one member of a pair of identical twins has major depression, the odds are about two in five that the other one will, too.

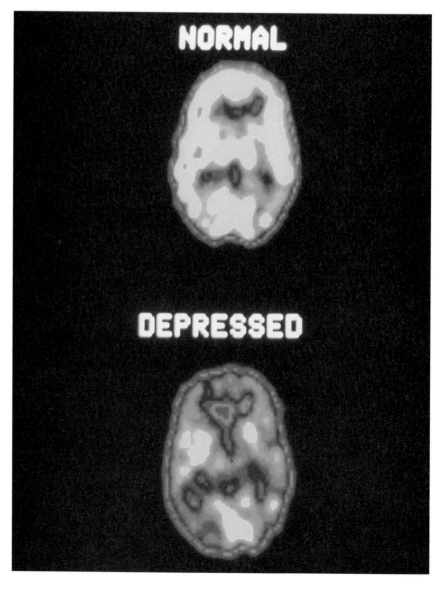

Positron emission tomography scans comparing a normal brain with that of someone with a depressed mental disorder. *(Reproduced by permission of Photo Researchers, Inc.)*

No one is quite sure why major depression affects more women than men. It could be that women, because of their monthly hormonal changes, are more biologically vulnerable. Another explanation might be that our society puts added pressures and limitations on women's lives, which could lead to feelings of helplessness and depression. One more explanation could be that women and men experience the same rate of depression, but that women are more open about their feelings and are more inclined to seek professional help if they have a problem.

Bipolar disorder

Another mood disorder is bipolar disorder (formerly called manic-depressive disorder). At first, bipolar disorder often seems to be depression. A person suffering from either of these disorders experiences periods of depression. However, in bipolar disorder, a person goes from periods of depression into periods of exaggerated elation (happiness), called mania. Manic people have excessive energy. They may feel exuberant, creative, and ready to take on the world. They often feel that they need little sleep and may even get only three or four hours of sleep during the manic episode. Other symptoms of mania include irritability, rapid and loud speech, and an inflated self-confidence.

Treatment

Medications known as antidepressants are considered standard therapy for depression. These medications raise the level of certain neurotransmitters in the body. Psychotherapy, used either alone or along with medication, is also an effective treatment for depression. Psychotherapy allows the psychiatrist to help a depressed person change his or her distorted views and beliefs about themselves and the world.

Both medication and psychotherapy typically take several weeks or months to become fully effective, and neither can help everyone. For those who are not helped, or whose symptoms are very severe, an alternative is electroconvulsive therapy (ECT; sometimes informally called shock therapy). In this therapy, electrodes are applied to the head (or to one side of the head) and the patient receives an electric shock strong enough to cause muscle spasms and convulsions.

The main drawback to ECT is temporary memory loss. Patients usually recover most of their missing memories within six to nine months. However, the few days immediately before the therapy are permanently lost. Since ECT can be a life-saving treatment for severely depressed people, it is appropriate when nothing else can provide help fast enough.

Bipolar disorder is most often treated with lithium, a natural mineral salt. While there has been a great deal of success in treating bipolar disorder patients with lithium and returning them to a normal life, researchers are not exactly sure how it works. It is a nonaddictive medication, but its dosage must be carefully monitored. Possible side effects of lithium therapy are stomachache, nausea, vomiting, diarrhea, hand tremors, thirst, fatigue, and muscle weakness.

Lithium therapy now allows many people with bipolar disorder to participate in ordinary everyday life. Seventy to 80 percent of bipolar patients respond well to lithium treatment without any serious side effects.

Desert

A desert is an arid land area that generally receives less than 10 inches (250 millimeters) of rainfall per year. What little water it does receive is quickly lost through evaporation. Average annual precipitation in the world's deserts ranges from about 0.4 to 1 inch (10 to 25 millimeters) in the driest areas to 10 inches (250 millimeters) in semiarid regions.

Other features that mark desert systems include high winds, low humidity, and temperatures that can fluctuate dramatically. It is not uncommon for the temperature to soar above 90°F (32°C) and then drop below 32°F (0°C) in a single day in the desert.

Most of the world's desert ecosystems (communities of plants and animals) are located in two belts near the tropics at 30 degrees north and 30 degrees south of the equator. These areas receive little rainfall because of the downward flow of dry air currents that originate at the equator. As this equatorial air moves north and south, it cools and loses whatever moisture it contains. Once this cool, dry air moves back toward Earth's surface, it is rewarmed, making it even drier. Over the desert areas, the dry air currents draw moisture away from the land on their journey back toward the equator.

Deserts around the world

The vast Sahara Desert in northern Africa encompasses an area 3,000 miles (4,800 kilometers) wide and 1,000 miles (1,600 kilometers) deep. Sand composes just 20 percent of the Sahara, while plains of rock, pebble, and salt flats, punctuated by mountains, make up the rest. The Sahara can experience temperatures that rise and fall 100°F (38°C) in a single day. Decades can go by without rain. By contrast, the Gobi Desert,

▼ Words to Know

Arid land: Land that receives less than 10 inches (250 millimeters) of rainfall annually and has a high rate of evaporation.

Desert pavement: Surface of flat desert lands covered with closely spaced, smooth rock fragments that resemble cobblestones.

Desert varnish: Dark film of iron oxide and manganese oxide on the surface of exposed desert rocks.

Rain-shadow deserts: Areas that lie in the shadow of mountain ranges and receive little precipitation.

covering 500,000 square miles (1,295,000 square kilometers) in north-central Asia, sits at a higher altitude than the Sahara. As a result, temperatures in the Gobi remain below freezing most of the year.

The Kalahari and Namib Deserts lie in the southern portion of Africa. The desert region that fills the interior of Australia is known as

Cactus in the Sonoran Desert in Organ Pipe Cactus National Park, Arizona. *(Reproduced by permission of The Stock Market.)*

the Outback. Antarctica, the land mass at the southern pole of the globe, is a polar desert. One of the driest places on Earth, it receives only a dusting of snow each year. Warmest summer temperatures in Antarctica reach only 25°F (−4°C).

The deserts of the United States are located at higher latitudes and in higher altitudes than is typical of many other arid regions of the world. Death Valley in California is both extremely arid and extremely hot in the summer. South of it are the relatively cooler and wetter Mojave and Sonoran Deserts.

Rain-shadow deserts

Rain-shadow deserts are those that lie in the shadow of mountain ranges. As air ascends on one side of a range, it releases any moisture it carries. Once on the other side, the air contains little moisture, forming deserts in the slope of the range. Among rain-shadow deserts are Death

Desert pavement at Race-track Playa in Death Valley, California. *(Reproduced by permission of JLM Visuals.)*

Desertification

Desertification refers to the gradual transformation of productive land into that with desertlike conditions. Desertification may occur in rain forests and tropical mountainous areas. Even a desert itself can become desertified, losing its sparse collection of plants and animals and becoming a barren wasteland.

Desertification occurs in response to continued land abuse, and may be brought about by natural or man-made actions. Among the natural forces are constant wind and water (which erode topsoil) and long-term changes in rainfall patterns (such as a drought). The list of human actions includes overgrazing of farm animals, strip mining, the depletion of groundwater supplies, the removal of forests, and the physical compacting of the soil (such as by cattle and off-road vehicles).

Almost 33 percent of Earth's land surface is desert, a proportion that is increasing by as much as 40 square miles (64 square kilometers) each day. The arid lands of North America are among those most affected by desertification: almost 90 percent are moderately to severely desertified.

Fortunately, scientists believe that severe desertification is rare. Many feel that most desertified areas can be restored to productivity through careful land management.

Valley (in the shadow of the Sierra Nevadas) and Argentina's Patagonian and Monte Deserts (in the shadow of Chile's Andes).

Desert topography

Dunes, wind-blown piles of sand, are the most common image of a desert landscape. Wind constantly sculpts sand piles into a wide variety of shapes. Dunes move as wind bounces sand up the dune's gently sloping windward side (facing the wind) to the peak of the slope. At the peak the wind's speed drops and sends sand cascading down the steeper lee side (downwind). As this process continues, the dune migrates in the direction the wind blows. Given enough sand and time, dunes override other dunes to thicknesses of thousands of feet, as in the Sahara Desert.

Sand carried by the wind can act as an abrasive on the land over which it flows. Rocks on the floor of a desert can become polished in this way. Closely spaced, smooth rock fragments that resemble cobblestones on the surface of flat lands are referred to as desert pavement. The dark film of iron oxide and manganese oxide on the surface of the exposed rocks is called desert varnish.

Life in the desert

The plants and animals that are able to survive the extremes of desert conditions have all evolved ways of compensating for the lack of water. Plants that are able to thrive in the desert include lichens (algae and fungi growing together). Lichens have no roots and can absorb water and nutrients from rain, dew, and the dust on which they grow. Succulent plants, such as cacti, quickly absorb rainwater when it comes and store it in their stems and leaves, if they have them. Other plants store nutrients in their roots and stems. Many desert shrubs have evolved into upside-down cone shapes. They collect large amounts of rain on their surfaces, then funnel it down to their bases.

Deserts are not lifeless, but are inhabited by insects, arachnids (spiders and scorpions), reptiles, birds, and mammals. Unlike plants, these animals can seek shelter from the scorching sun, cold, and winds by crawling into underground burrows. Many have adapted to the harsh desert environment by developing specific body processes. Some small mammals, such as rodents, excrete only concentrated urine and dry feces, and perspire little as a way of conserving body fluids. The camel's body temperature can soar to 105°F (41°C) before this mammal sweats. It can lose up to one-third of its body weight and replace it at a single drinking.

[See also **Biome**]

Diabetes mellitus

Diabetes mellitus is a disease caused by the body's inability to use the hormone insulin. Insulin is normally produced in the pancreas, a gland attached to the small intestine. Its function is to convert carbohydrates into glucose. Glucose (also known as blood sugar) is the compound used by cells to obtain the energy they need to survive, reproduce, and carry out all their normal functions.

When cells are unable to use glucose for these functions, they use fat instead. One product of the metabolism of fats is a group of compounds known as ketones. Ketones tend to collect in the blood and disrupt brain functions.

▼ Words to Know

Glucose: A simple sugar that serves as the source of energy for cells.

Hormone: Chemicals that regulate various body functions.

Insulin-dependent diabetes: Also known as juvenile or Type I diabetes; a form of diabetes that requires the daily injection of insulin.

Ketones: Organic compounds formed during the breakdown of fats that can have harmful effects on the brain.

Noninsulin-dependent diabetes: Also known as adult-onset or Type II diabetes; a form of diabetes that is often caused by obesity and can be controlled by diet, exercise, and oral medication rather than daily injections of insulin.

Pancreas: The organ responsible for secreting insulin.

Common signs of diabetes are excessive thirst, urination, and fatigue. The long-term effects of diabetes include loss of vision, decreased blood supply to the hands and feet and pain. If left untreated, diabetes can produce coma and cause death.

Types

Two types of diabetes mellitus are known. Type I diabetes is also called juvenile or insulin-dependent diabetes. Type I diabetes occurs when the pancreas fails to produce enough insulin. Type II diabetes is also called adult-onset or noninsulin-dependent diabetes. Type II diabetes results when the pancreas does produce insulin but, for some reason, the body is unable to use the insulin normally. Type I diabetes can usually be controlled by doses of insulin and a strict diet. Type II diabetes is often caused by obesity and is usually controlled by diet alone.

Incidence

More than 12 million Americans are affected by diabetes. An annual increase of about 5 percent in the disease is attributed both to the population's increased rate of longevity and a rising rate of obesity. Experts believe that for each reported new case of diabetes, there is an unreported one because symptoms of the early stages of adult diabetes tend to go unrecognized. Symptoms usually progress from mild to severe as the disease progresses.

Approximately 300,000 deaths each year in the United States are attributed to diabetes. Its prevalence increases with age, from about 0.2 percent in persons under 17 years of age to about 10 percent in persons aged 65 years and over. Females have a higher rate of incidence for the disease, while higher income groups in the United States show a lesser incidence than lower income groups. The incident rate is markedly different among ethnic groups. It is 20 percent higher in non-Caucasians than in Caucasians. However, for reasons as yet unknown, the rate of diabetes in ethnic groups such as Native Americans, Latin Americans, and Asian Americans is especially high and continues to rise.

History

The symptoms of diabetes were identified 3,500 years ago in Egypt and were also known in ancient India, China, Japan, and Rome. The Persian physician Avicenna (980–1037) described the disease and its consequences. The English epidemiologist Thomas Willis (1621–1675) was the first modern physician to discover that the urine of diabetics tasted sweet. This characteristic of the disease explains its name since diabetes refers to the frequent urination associated with the condition and mellitus refers to the honeylike taste of the urine.

The role of insulin in the metabolism of glucose was first suggested by the English physiologist Edward Sharpey-Schäfer (1850–1935) in 1916. Five years later, insulin was first isolated by the Canadian physiologists Frederick Banting (1891–1941) and Charles Best (1899–1978). In 1922, Banting and Best first used insulin to successfully treat a diabetic patient, 14-year-old Leonard Thompson, of Toronto, Ontario.

Diagnosis

Diagnosis is the process of identifying a disease or disorder in a person by examining the person and studying the results of medical tests.

The process of diagnosis begins when a patient appears before a doctor with a set of symptoms, such as pain, nausea, fever, or some other unusual feeling. In many cases, the diagnosis is relatively simple. The physician can decide by making a few simple observations as to the patient's problem and can prescribe a proper treatment. At other times, the

Words to Know

Benign: Noncancerous.

Biopsy: The removal and examination of tissue from a person's body.

Invasive: A technique that involves entering the body.

Laparoscope: A device consisting of a long flexible tube that contains a light source that allows a physician to look into the abdominal cavity without making a large incision in the abdominal wall.

Laparotomy: A process by which the abdominal wall is opened in order to allow a physician to look inside.

Malignant: Cancerous.

Palpation: A technique used by doctors that involves the use of fingers to touch and feel various parts of a patient's body.

Stethoscope: A device that magnifies sounds produced in the human body.

symptoms may be more difficult to interpret, and making a diagnosis may require laboratory tests and other kinds of examinations.

Sources of information

In order to make a diagnosis, a physician searches for information from three major sources: the patient himself or herself, a physical examination, and a laboratory examination.

Patient information. Patient information is obtained by asking the patient a variety of questions about his or her previous health history and present symptoms. For example, the patient who is experiencing unusual pains may be asked to tell how long the pains have persisted, where they are located, the type of pain experienced, and whether the pain is constant or intermittent.

A patient's occupation may have a bearing on his or her illness. Perhaps he or she works around chemicals that may cause illness. A job that requires repeated bending and lifting may result in muscle strain or back pain. A police officer or fire fighter may have periods of boredom interrupted by periods of stress or fear.

The medical history of a patient's family may also be helpful. Some diseases are hereditary and some, although not hereditary, are more likely to occur if the patient's parent or other close relative has had such a disease. For example, the person whose father has had a heart attack is more likely to have a heart attack than is a person whose family has been free of heart disease.

Personal habits, such as smoking or drinking large amounts of alcohol, also contribute to disease. Lack of exercise, lack of sleep, and an unhealthy diet are all involved in bringing about symptoms of disease.

The physical examination.   In addition to exploring the patient's clinical history, the physician will carry out a physical examination to further narrow the list of possible medical problems. The patient's temperature, blood pressure, and rate of respiration will be measured. He or she will be weighed and his or her height measured. The physician will examine the eardrums and look into the throat for signs of inflammation, infection, or other abnormal conditions.

The heart and lungs can be examined superficially (from outside the body) using a stethoscope. A stethoscope allows the physician to hear abnormalities in the heartbeat or in the functioning of the heart valves. The presence of water or other fluid in the lungs can also be heard with a stethoscope. The physician can also study sounds made by the intestines by listening to them through the stethoscope.

A physician may also use a technique called palpation, in which the physician uses his or her fingers to probe the abdomen for signs of pain or an abnormal lump or growth. The doctor also feels the neck, the area under the armpit, and other areas to locate any enlarged lymph nodes, a sign of an infection. Such probing also may bring to light the presence of a tender area previously unknown to the patient.

If the patient is complaining of an injury, the physician can carefully palpate around the injury to determine its size. He or she can bend a leg or arm to determine whether a joint has been broken. Similar techniques also reveal whether a ligament (tissue that connects bones) has been torn and if it may need surgical correction.

The laboratory examination.   The physician also may decide to have laboratory tests performed on various fluids taken from the patient. The most common fluids used are blood, urine, stomach fluid, and spinal fluid. As an example, tests of the blood reveal the number of white and red blood cells. An elevated number of white blood cells indicates an infection is present, but does not pinpoint the location of the infection. Blood also carries hormones and other components that are directly affected by disease or inflammation.

The modern clinical laboratory is one of automation and high technology. At one time, a laboratory technician was required to mix together the chemicals needed for each clinical test. Newer technology requires only that a blood specimen be placed in one end of a machine. The blood is carried through the machine, where minute amounts of the chemicals are added as needed, and test results are printed out automatically. This technology also enables the measurement of blood or urine components in amounts much smaller than previous technology allowed. In some cases, a single microgram (one-millionth of a gram) can be detected in blood, urine or some other fluid.

The physician also may want to obtain X rays of an injured area to rule out the possibility of a fractured bone. (X rays are a form of electromagnetic radiation that can penetrate solids. They are used to generate images of bones and other tissues.) The presence of a heart condition can often be determined by taking an electrocardiogram (ECG), which measures the electrical activity of the heart. Changes in an ECG can indicate the presence of heart disease or give evidence of a past heart attack. CAT (computerized axial tomography) scans use X rays to produce images of one layer of hard or soft tissue, a procedure useful in detecting small

A physician recording his diagnosis on audiotape while viewing a patient's chest X ray. *(Reproduced by permission of The Stock Market.)*

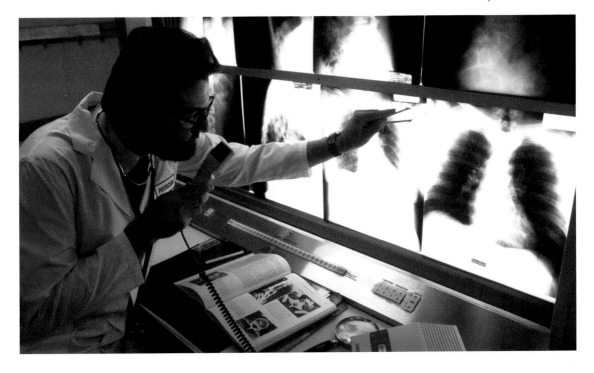

tumors. Magnetic resonance imaging (MRI) uses radio waves in a magnetic field to generate images of a layer of the brain, heart, or other organ. Ultrasound waves are also sometimes used to detect tumors.

Other laboratory specimens can be obtained by invasive techniques. An invasive technique is one in which a physician cuts open the body to look directly inside it for possible medical problems. For example, a physician who finds a suspicious lump or swelling can remove part of the lump and send it to the laboratory to be examined. The surgical removal of tissue for testing is called a biopsy. In the laboratory, the specimen is sliced very thinly, dyed to highlight differences in tissues, and examined under the microscope. This procedure enables the physician to determine whether the lump is malignant (cancerous) or benign (noncancerous).

The method of actually looking into the body cavity used to consist of a major surgical procedure called a laparotomy. In that procedure, an incision is made in the abdomen so the physician can look at each organ and other internal structures in order to determine the presence of disease or a parasite. Today, the laparotomy is carried out using a flexible tube called a laparoscope. The laparoscope is inserted into the body through a small incision. It is attached to a television monitor that gives the physician an enlarged view of the inside of the body. The flexibility of the laparoscope allows the instrument to be guided around the organs. A light attached to the scope helps the physician see each organ. The laparoscope is also equipped with a tiny device to collect specimens or to suction blood out of the abdomen.

Dialysis

Dialysis is a process by which small molecules in a solution are separated from large molecules. Dialysis has a number of important commercial and industrial applications and plays a crucial role in maintaining the health of humans. For some people, in fact, the term dialysis refers to a specific kind of medical treatment in which a machine (the dialysis machine) takes on the functions of a human kidney. Dialysis machines have made possible the survival of thousands of people who would otherwise have died as a result of kidney failure.

Dialysis is a specific example of a more general process known as diffusion. Diffusion was first described by Scottish chemist Thomas Graham (1805–1869) around 1861. Graham studied the movement of molecules of different sizes through a semipermeable membrane. (A semipermeable membrane is a thin sheet of material that allows some substances to pass through—or diffuse—but not others.) Many tissues in the human body are semipermeable membranes. Graham discovered that some substances, such as the sodium and chloride ions of which ordinary table salt is composed, diffuse through a semipermeable membrane up to 50 times as fast as other substances, such as ordinary table sugar.

Today we know the reason behind Graham's observation. Semipermeable membranes are not actually solid sheets of material. Instead, they contain tiny holes too small to be seen by the unaided eye. Those holes are just large enough to allow tiny particles like sodium and chloride ions to pass through, but they are too small to permit the passage of large molecules, such as those of sugar.

In a typical dialysis experiment, a bag made of a semipermeable membrane is filled with a solution to be dialyzed. The bag is then suspended in a stream of running water. Small particles in the solution within the bag gradually diffuse across the semipermeable membrane and are carried away by the running water. Larger molecules are essentially retained within the bag. By this process, a highly efficient separation of substances can be achieved.

Kidney dialysis

The kidney is a dialyzing organ. Blood that enters the kidney has a great variety of materials in it; some are essential (important, necessary) to human life, others are harmful to life. Proteins circulating in the blood, for example, have many critical bodily functions, such as protecting against disease and carrying "messages" from one part of the body to another. But other materials in blood are waste products of bodily functions that must be eliminated. If they remained in blood, they would cause illness or death. Urea, formed during the breakdown of proteins, is one such compound.

Blood that passes through the kidney is dialyzed to separate essential compounds from harmful compounds. Protein molecules are too large to go through semipermeable membranes in the kidney and are retained in the blood. Urea molecules are much smaller than protein molecules. They pass through those membranes and into urine, in which they are excreted from the body.

The dialysis machine. Sometimes a person's kidneys may be damaged by disease or physical injury. They are no longer able to dialyze blood properly. At one time, people in this situation died because of the accumulation of poisonous materials (such as urea) in their blood.

Then, in the 1910s, scientists invented an artificial kidney machine that could be used to dialyze blood. A pioneer in this research was American biochemist John Jacob Abel (1857–1938).

In the kidney machine, blood is removed from a person's arm, passed through a dialyzing system, and then returned to the patient. The machine functions much as a natural kidney would—with one important exception. A natural kidney has a mechanism known as reverse dialysis for returning to the body certain small molecules (primarily glucose) that should not be excreted. The kidney machine is unable to do so, and glucose that it removes must be replaced by intravenous injection.

Electrodialysis

Another form of dialysis is known as electrodialysis. In electrodialysis, an electrical field is set up around a dialysis apparatus. The electrical field causes charged particles in a solution to pass through the semipermeable membrane more quickly than they would without the field. Any large molecules in the solution, though, remain where they are.

One possible application of electrodialysis is the desalination of water. In this procedure, sodium ions and chloride ions from the salt in seawater are forced out, leaving pure water behind.

[See also **Diffusion**]

Diesel engine

A diesel engine is a type of internal-combustion engine developed by German engineer Rudolf Diesel (1858–1913) in the late nineteenth century. His original design called for the use of coal dust as fuel, but most modern diesel engines burn low-cost fuel oil. Whereas gasoline engines (found in the majority of present-day automobiles) use an electric spark to ignite the premixed fuel-air blend, diesel engines use compressed air to ignite the fuel.

In both gasoline and diesel engines, fuel is ignited in a cylinder, or chamber. Inside the sealed, hollow cylinder is a piston (a solid cylinder) that is attached at the bottom to a crankshaft. The movement of the piston up and down turns the crankshaft, which transfers that movement through various gears to the drive wheels in an automobile.

In a diesel engine cylinder, the piston completes one up-and-down cycle in four strokes: intake, compression, power, and exhaust. During the intake stroke, the piston moves downward, sucking air into the cylinder through an open intake valve. On the compression stroke, the intake valve closes and the piston rises, compressing the air in the cylinder and causing it to become heated. While the air is being compressed, a fuel pump sprays fuel into the cylinder to mix with the air. When the compressed, hot air reaches the right temperature, it ignites the fuel, driving the piston down on the power stroke. As the piston rises on the exhaust stroke, the exhaust valve opens and the gases created by explosion of the fuel (exhaust) pass out of the cylinder. Then the cycle repeats.

The entire combustion cycle takes but a fraction of a second. Diesel engines can operate from several hundred up to almost one thousand revolutions per minute. The high pressure created in the cylinders during compression requires diesel engines to be strongly constructed and, thus, much heavier than gasoline engines. This weight cuts into their fuel efficiency. Diesel engines also emit high levels of foul-smelling exhaust.

However, diesel engines are more powerful than conventional gasoline engines and run on a less costly fuel. First installed on a ship in 1910 and in an automobile in 1922, they are generally used in large vehicles such as locomotives, trucks, and buses, and in heavy construction and agricultural machinery. Because of their ability to burn crude fuels while delivering an efficient amount of the fuel's energy as usable power, diesel engines are almost the only choice for industrial power throughout the world.

[See also **Internal-combustion engine**]

The combustion cycle of the diesel engine. (Reproduced by permission of The Gale Group.)

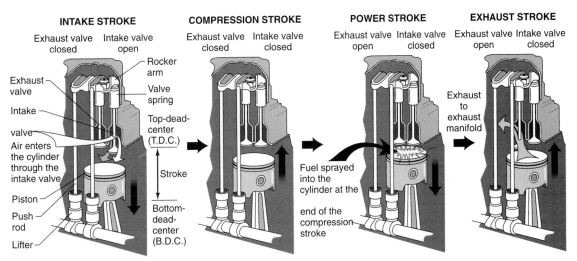

INTAKE STROKE — COMPRESSION STROKE — POWER STROKE — EXHAUST STROKE

Diffraction

Diffraction is the bending of waves (such as light waves or sound waves) as they pass around an obstacle or through an opening. Anyone who has watched ocean waves entering a bay or harbor has probably witnessed diffraction. As the waves strike the first point of land, they change direction. Instead of moving into the bay or harbor parallel to (in the same direction as) land, they travel at an angle to it. The narrower the opening, the more dramatic the effect. As waves enter a narrow harbor opening, such as San Francisco's Golden Gate, they change from a parallel set of wave fronts to a fan-shaped pattern.

The diffraction of light has many important applications. For example, a device known as the diffraction grating is used to break white light apart into its colored components. Patterns produced by diffraction gratings provide information about the kind of light that falls on them.

Fundamentals

All waves are subject to diffraction when they encounter an obstacle in their path. Consider the shadow of a flagpole cast by the Sun on the ground. From a distance the darkened zone of the shadow gives the

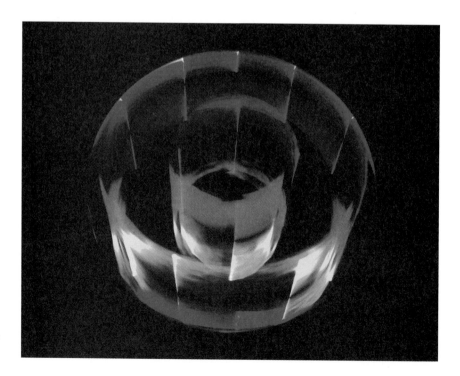

Circular diffraction pattern.
(Reproduced by permission of Photo Researchers, Inc.)

Words to Know

Diffraction pattern: The wave pattern observed after a wave has passed through a diffracting aperture (or opening).

Frequency: The number of segments in a wave that pass a given point every second.

Interference pattern: Alternating bands of light and dark that result from the mixing of two waves.

Wavelength: The distance between two identical parts of a wave, such as two consecutive crests of the wave.

X-ray diffraction: A method used for studying the structure of crystals.

impression that light traveling in a straight line from the Sun was blocked by the pole. But careful observation of the shadow's edge will reveal that the change from dark to light is not abrupt. Instead, there is a gray area along the edge that was created by light that was bent—or diffracted—at the side of the pole.

When a source of waves, such as a lightbulb, sends a beam through an opening, or aperture, a diffraction pattern will appear on a screen placed behind the aperture. The diffraction pattern will look something like the aperture (perhaps a slit, a circle, or a square) but it will be surrounded by some diffracted waves that give it a fuzzy appearance.

The diffraction that occurs depends primarily on two variables: the wavelength of the wave and the size of the opening or aperture through which the waves pass. (Wavelength is defined as the distance between two identical parts of a wave, such as two consecutive crests of a wave. The only difference between waves of light, waves of radar, waves of X rays, and of many other kinds of waves is their wavelength—and their frequency, which depends on their wavelength.) The wavelength of light, for example, is in the range of 400 to 700 nanometers (billionths of a meter). In comparison, the wavelength of radar waves ranges from about 0.1 to 1 meter.

When the wavelength of a wave is much smaller than the aperture through which it travels, the observed diffraction is small. A beam of light traveling through a window, for example, has a wavelength many trillions of times smaller than the window opening. It would be difficult to observe diffraction in this situation. But a beam of light passing through a tiny pin hole produces a different effect. In this case, a diffraction pattern can be seen quite clearly.

Applications

Diffraction gratings. A diffraction grating is a tool whose operation is based on the diffraction of light. It consists of a flat plate (usually made of glass or plastic) into which are etched thousands of thin slits or grooves. The accuracy of the grating depends on the grooves' being parallel to each other, equally spaced, and equal in width.

When light strikes a diffraction grating, it is diffracted by each of the thousands of grooves individually. The diffracted waves that are produced then mix or interfere with each other in different ways, depending on the source of the light beam. Light from a sodium vapor lamp, from a mercury (fluorescent) lamp, and from an incandescent lamp all produce different light patterns in a diffraction grating.

Scientists have recorded the kind of light pattern (spectrum) produced when each of the different chemical elements is heated and its light shined on a diffraction grating. In studying the light of an unknown object (such as a star), then, the diffraction grating spectrum can be compared to the known spectra of elements. In this way, elements in the unknown object can be identified.

X-ray diffraction. In the 1910s, William Henry (1862–1942) and William Lawrence Bragg (1890–1971), a father-and-son team of English physicists, had an interesting idea for using diffraction. They set out to find the very finest diffraction grating anyone could imagine and decided that a crystal—such as a crystal of ordinary table salt—fit the bill. The atoms and ions that make up a crystal are arranged in the same way as the grooves of a diffraction grating. Crystalline atoms and ions are laid out in very orderly rows at exactly the same distance from each other, as is the case with a diffraction grating. But the size of the "grooves" in a crystal (the space between atoms and ions) is much smaller than in any human-made diffraction grating.

The Braggs set to work experimenting with crystals and diffraction. Unfortunately, the wavelength of a light wave was too large to be diffracted by atoms and ions in a crystal. But X rays—which have a much smaller wavelength than light waves—would diffract perfectly off rows of atoms or ions in a crystal.

When the Braggs shined X rays off various crystals, they made a fascinating discovery. For each type of crystal studied, a unique pattern of fuzzy circles was produced. X rays had been diffracted according to the ways in which atoms or ions were arranged in the crystal. The Braggs had discovered a method for determining how atoms or ions are arranged in a given crystal. That method, known as X-ray crystallography, is now one of the most powerful tools available to chemists for analyzing the structure of substances.

[*See also* **Hologram and holography; Wave motion**]

Diffusion

Diffusion is the movement of molecules from a region of high concentration to one of low concentration. If you have ever opened a bottle of cologne or perfume, you have witnessed diffusion. Molecules of the scent escape from the container, where they are present in very high concentration. They spread outward in every direction to regions where they are in low concentration. Your nose is able to detect the smell of the cologne or perfume even if you are quite a distance from the bottle that has been opened.

Diffusion occurs in all states of matter: solid, liquid, and gas. It occurs rapidly enough to be observable in a reasonable period of time, however, only in liquids and gases.

You can demonstrate diffusion easily in your home. Fill a glass with water. Then add 10 drops of ink (any color) to the water very carefully. The ink sinks to the bottom of the glass because it is more dense than water. Place the glass in a place where it will not be disturbed and make observations of it every day. Over time, the colored ink at the bottom of the glass spreads upward. It moves from a region of high concentration to one of low concentration.

Eventually, the water in the glass is the same shade: a grey, light blue, or pink throughout. The original black, blue, or red ink has been diluted with water to produce the paler shade. Diffusion eventually stops because no region of high ink concentration remains. The concentration of ink and water is the same throughout the glass. That rule applies to all cases of diffusion. When differences in concentration no longer exist, diffusion stops.

Osmosis

Osmosis is diffusion through a membrane. The membrane acts as a barrier between two solutions of different concentration. One substance (usually water) travels from an area of high concentration to one of low concentration. Osmosis can be compared to the examples of diffusion given above involving perfume and ink. In those cases, no barrier was present to separate perfume from air or ink from water. Diffusion took place directly between two materials.

In contrast, a barrier is always present with osmosis. That barrier is usually called a semipermeable membrane because it allows some kinds of materials to pass through, but not others.

The most familiar example of osmosis through a semipermeable membrane may be a living cell. Cells contain semipermeable membranes

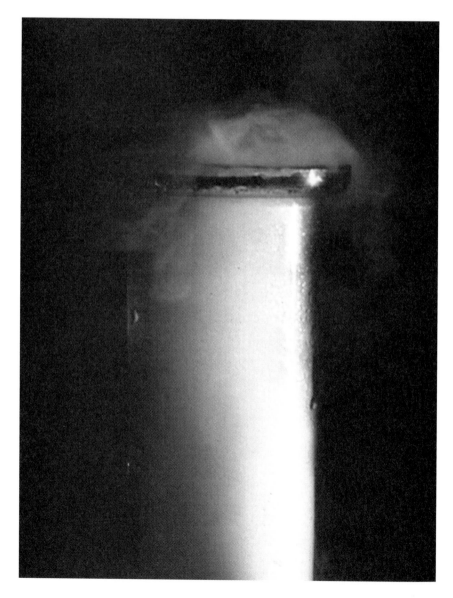

Carbon dioxide vapor diffusing from an open gas jar. The vapor molecules are traveling from the area of high concentration (the jar) to the area of low concentration (the open air). *(Reproduced by permission of Photo Researchers, Inc.)*

that act something like a plastic baggy holding cell contents inside. The cell membrane is not a solid material, however, but a thin sheet containing many tiny holes. (Imagine a self-sealing sandwich bag—its surface dotted with minuscule holes—then filled with water.) The holes allow small molecules and ions (such as molecules of water and sodium ions) to pass through, but trap larger molecules (such as proteins) inside the cell.

[*See also* **Dialysis**]

Digestive system

The digestive system is a group of organs responsible for the conversion of food into nutrients and energy needed by the body. In humans, the digestive system consists of the mouth, esophagus, stomach, and small and large intestines. The digestive tube made up by these organs is known as the alimentary canal.

Several glands—salivary glands, liver, gall bladder, and pancreas—also play a part in digestion. These glands secrete digestive juices containing enzymes that break down the food chemically into smaller molecules that are more easily absorbed by the body. The digestive system also separates and disposes of waste products ingested with the food.

Ingestion

Food taken into the mouth is first broken down into smaller pieces by the teeth. The tongue then rolls these pieces into balls called boluses. Together, the sensations of sight, taste, and smell of the food cause the salivary glands, located in the mouth, to produce saliva. An enzyme in the saliva called amylase begins the breakdown of carbohydrates (starch) into simple sugars.

The bolus, which is now a battered, moistened, and partially digested ball of food, is swallowed, moving to the pharynx (throat) at the back of the mouth. In the pharynx, rings of muscles force the food into the esophagus, the first part of the upper digestive tube. The esophagus extends from the bottom part of the throat to the upper part of the stomach.

The esophagus does not take part in digestion. Its job is to move the bolus into the stomach. Food is moved through the esophagus (and other parts of the alimentary canal) by a wavelike muscular motion known as

▼ Words to Know

Alimentary canal: Tube formed by the pharynx, esophagus, stomach, and intestines through which food passes.

Amylase: Digestive enzyme that breaks down carbohydrates to simple sugars.

Bile: Bitter, greenish liquid produced in the liver and stored in the gall bladder that dissolves fats.

Bolus: Battered, moistened, and partially digested ball of food that passes from the mouth to the stomach.

Carbohydrate: A compound consisting of carbon, hydrogen, and oxygen found in plants and used as a food by humans and other animals.

Chyme: Thick liquid of partially digested food passed from the stomach to the small intestine.

Enzyme: Any of numerous complex proteins that are produced by living cells and spark specific biochemical reactions.

Esophagitis: Commonly known as heartburn, an inflammation of the esophagus caused by gastric acids flowing back into the esophagus.

Gastric juice: Digestive juice produced by the stomach wall that contains hydrochloric acid and the enzyme pepsin.

Pepsin: Digestive enzyme that breaks down protein.

Peristalsis: Wavelike motion of the digestive system that moves food through the system.

Proteins: Large molecules that are essential to the structure and functioning of all living cells.

Ulcer: Inflamed sore or lesion on the skin or a mucous membrane of the body.

Villi: Fingerlike projections found in the small intestine that increase the absorption area of the intestine.

peristalsis (pronounced pear-i-STALL-sis). This motion consists of the alternate contraction and relaxation of the smooth muscles lining the tract.

At the junction of the esophagus and stomach there is a powerful muscle—the esophageal sphincter—that acts as a valve to keep food and stomach acids from flowing back into the esophagus and mouth.

Digestion in the stomach

Chemical digestion begins in the stomach. The stomach is a large, hollow, pouched-shaped muscular organ. Food in the stomach is broken down by the action of gastric juice, which contains hydrochloric acid and pepsin (an enzyme that digests protein). The stomach begins its production of gastric juice while food is still in the mouth. Nerves from the cheeks and tongue are stimulated and send messages to the brain. The brain in turn sends messages to nerves in the stomach wall, stimulating the secretion of gastric juice before the arrival of food. The second signal for gastric juice production occurs when food arrives in the stomach and touches the lining.

Gastric juice is secreted from the linings of the stomach walls, along with mucus that helps to protect the stomach lining from the action of the acid. Three layers of powerful stomach muscles churn food into a thick liquid called chyme (pronounced KIME). From time to time, chyme is passed through the pyloric sphincter, the opening between the stomach and the small intestine.

Digestion and absorption in the small intestine

The small intestine is a long, narrow tube running from the stomach to the large intestine. The small intestine is greatly coiled and twisted. Its full length is about 20 feet (6 meters). The small intestine is subdivided into three sections: the duodenum (pronounced do-o-DEE-num), the jejunum (pronounced je-JOO-num), and the ileum (pronounced ILL-ee-um).

The duodenum is about 10 inches (25 centimeters) long and connects with the lower portion of the stomach. When chyme reaches the duodenum, it is further broken down by intestinal juices and through the action of the pancreas and gall bladder. The pancreas is a large gland located below the stomach that secretes pancreatic juice into the duodenum through the pancreatic duct. There are three enzymes in pancreatic juice that break down carbohydrates, fats, and proteins. The gall bladder, located next to the liver, stores bile produced by the liver. While bile does not contain enzymes, it contains bile salts that help to dissolve fats. The gall bladder empties bile into the duodenum when chyme enters that portion of the intestine.

The jejunum is about 8.2 feet (2.5 meters) long. The digested carbohydrates, fats, proteins, and most of the vitamins, minerals, and iron are absorbed in this section. The inner lining of the small intestine is composed of up to five million tiny, fingerlike projections called villi. The villi increase the rate of absorption of nutrients into the bloodstream by greatly increasing the surface area of the small intestine.

The ileum, the last section of the small intestine, is the longest, measuring 11 feet (3.4 meters). Certain vitamins and other nutrients are absorbed here.

Absorption and elimination in the large intestine

The large intestine is wider and heavier than the small intestine. However, it is much shorter—only about 5 feet (1.5 meters) long. It rises up on the right side of the body (the ascending colon), crosses over to the other side underneath the stomach (the transverse colon), descends on the left side, (the descending colon), then forms an s-shape (the sigmoid colon) before reaching the rectum and anus. The muscular rectum, about 6 inches (16 centimeters) long, expels feces (stool) through the anus, which has a large muscular sphincter that controls the passage of waste matter.

The large intestine removes water from the waste products of digestion and returns some of it to the bloodstream. Fecal matter contains undigested food, bacteria, and cells from the walls of the digestive tract. Millions of bacteria in the large intestine help to produce certain B vitamins and vitamin K. These vitamins are absorbed into the bloodstream along with the water.

Disorders of the digestive system

Among the several disorders that affect the digestive system are esophagitis (heartburn) and ulcers. Esophagitis is an inflammation of the esophagus caused by gastric acids flowing back into the esophagus. Mild cases of this condition are usually treated with commercial antacids.

Stomach ulcers are sores that form in the lining of the stomach. They may vary in size from a small sore to a deep cavity. Ulcers that form in the lining of the stomach and the duodenum are called peptic ulcers because they need stomach acid and the enzyme pepsin to form. Duodenal ulcers are the most common type. They tend to be smaller than stomach ulcers and heal more quickly. Any ulcer that heals leaves a scar.

Until the early 1990s, the medical community generally believed that ulcers were caused by several factors, including stress and a poor diet. However, medical researchers soon came to believe that a certain bacterium that can live undetected in the mucous lining of the stomach was responsible. This bacterium irritated and weakened the lining, making it more susceptible to damage by stomach acids.

Opposite Page: The human digestive process. (Reproduced by permission of The Gale Group.)

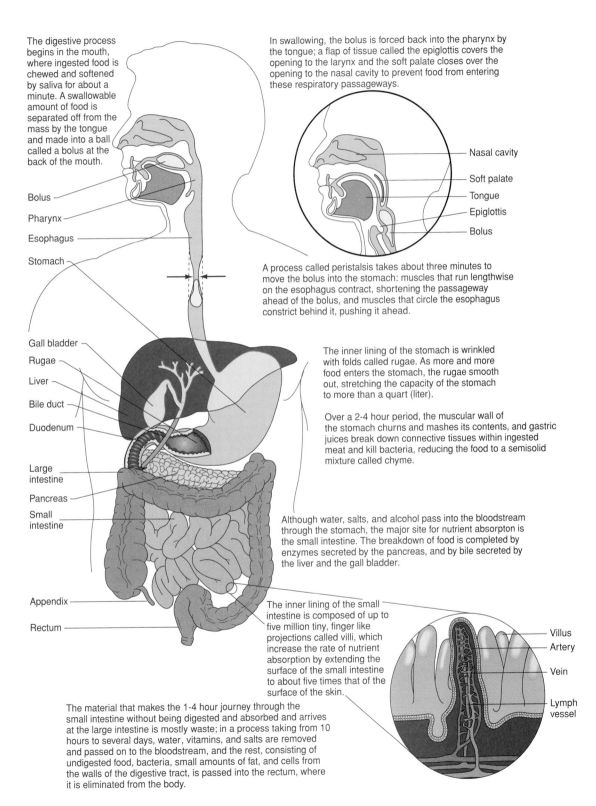

The digestive process begins in the mouth, where ingested food is chewed and softened by saliva for about a minute. A swallowable amount of food is separated off from the mass by the tongue and made into a ball called a bolus at the back of the mouth.

Bolus

Pharynx

Esophagus

Stomach

In swallowing, the bolus is forced back into the pharynx by the tongue; a flap of tissue called the epiglottis covers the opening to the larynx and the soft palate closes over the opening to the nasal cavity to prevent food from entering these respiratory passageways.

Nasal cavity

Soft palate

Tongue

Epiglottis

Bolus

A process called peristalsis takes about three minutes to move the bolus into the stomach: muscles that run lengthwise on the esophagus contract, shortening the passageway ahead of the bolus, and muscles that circle the esophagus constrict behind it, pushing it ahead.

Gall bladder

Rugae

Liver

Bile duct

Duodenum

Large intestine

Pancreas

Small intestine

The inner lining of the stomach is wrinkled with folds called rugae. As more and more food enters the stomach, the rugae smooth out, stretching the capacity of the stomach to more than a quart (liter).

Over a 2-4 hour period, the muscular wall of the stomach churns and mashes its contents, and gastric juices break down connective tissues within ingested meat and kill bacteria, reducing the food to a semisolid mixture called chyme.

Although water, salts, and alcohol pass into the bloodstream through the stomach, the major site for nutrient absorption is the small intestine. The breakdown of food is completed by enzymes secreted by the pancreas, and by bile secreted by the liver and the gall bladder.

Appendix

Rectum

The inner lining of the small intestine is composed of up to five million tiny, finger like projections called villi, which increase the rate of nutrient absorption by extending the surface of the small intestine to about five times that of the surface of the skin.

Villus

Artery

Vein

Lymph vessel

The material that makes the 1-4 hour journey through the small intestine without being digested and absorbed and arrives at the large intestine is mostly waste; in a process taking from 10 hours to several days, water, vitamins, and salts are removed and passed on to the bloodstream, and the rest, consisting of undigested food, bacteria, small amounts of fat, and cells from the walls of the digestive tract, is passed into the rectum, where it is eliminated from the body.

It is believed that about 80 percent of stomach ulcers may be caused by the bacterial infection. With this discovery, ulcer patients today are being treated with antibiotics and antacids rather than special diets or expensive medicines.

Dinosaur

Dinosaurs are a group of now-extinct, terrestrial reptiles in the order Dinosauria. They lived during the Mesozoic Era, from about 225 million years ago to 66 million years ago. Species of dinosaurs ranged from chicken-sized creatures such as the 2-pound (1-kilogram) predator *Compsognathus* to colossal, herbivorous animals known as sauropods weighing more than 80 tons (72 metric tons). The sauropods were larger than any terrestrial animals that lived before or since.

Some dinosaurs were enormous, awesomely fierce predators, while others were mild-mannered plant eaters. The word dinosaur is derived from two Greek words meaning "terrible lizard." The name comes from the fact that the remains of the earliest dinosaurs discovered were very large and showed they had a lizardlike appearance.

Biology of the dinosaurs

The dinosaurs shared some common physical characteristics, such as the presence of two openings on opposite sides of their skulls and 25 vertebrae. However, the dinosaurs also differed from each other in many important ways. They displayed an enormous range of forms and functions, and they filled a wide array of ecological niches. Some of the dinosaurs were, in fact, quite bizarre in their shape and, undoubtedly, their behavior.

Most species of dinosaurs had a long tail and long neck, but this was not the case for all species. Most of the dinosaurs walked on their four legs, although some species were bipedal, using only their rear legs for locomotion. Their forelegs were greatly reduced in size and probably used only for grasping. The species that walked on four legs were all peaceful herbivores. In contrast, many of the bipedal dinosaurs were fast-running predators.

The teeth of dinosaur species were highly diverse. Many species were exclusively herbivorous, and their teeth were correspondingly adapted for cutting and grinding vegetation. Other dinosaurs were fierce predators, and their teeth were shaped like serrated (notched) knives. These teeth were undoubtedly used to seize and stab their prey, cutting it into smaller pieces that could be swallowed whole.

Words to Know

Bipedal: Walking on two feet.

Carnivore (carnivorous): Meat-eating.

Embryo: The earliest stage of animal development in the uterus before the animal is considered a fetus.

Extinct: No longer alive on Earth.

Fossil: Evidence of plant or animal life preserved in earth, usually in rocks.

Herbivore (herbivorous): Plant-eating.

Ornithischian dinosaurs: Dinosaurs with birdlike characteristics.

Predator: An animal that eats other animals.

Saurischian dinosaurs: Dinosaurs with reptilelike characteristics.

Sauropods: A group of large saurischian herbivores.

Terrestrial: Relating to the land.

Thecodonts: Early reptiles regarded as ancestors of the dinosaurs.

Until recently, it was widely believed that dinosaurs were rather stupid, slow-moving, cold-blooded creatures. However, some scientists now believe that dinosaurs were intelligent, social, quick-moving, and probably warm-blooded animals. This question is still rather controversial. Scientists have not yet reached agreement as to whether at least some of the dinosaurs were able to regulate their body temperature by producing heat through metabolic reactions.

Evidence for the existence of dinosaurs

Humans have never lived at the same time as dinosaurs on Earth. Yet, a surprising amount is known about these remarkable reptiles. Evidence about the existence and nature of dinosaurs has been obtained from fossilized traces left by these animals in sediment deposits.

The first evidence suggesting the existence of dinosaurs was the discovery of traces of their ancient footprints in sedimentary rocks. Sedimentary rocks are formed when sand, silt, clay and other materials are packed together under great pressure. Dinosaurs left their footprints in soft mud as they moved along a marine shore or riverbank. That mud was subsequently covered over as a new layer of sediment accumulated, and later solidified into rock. Under very rare circumstances, this process preserved traces of the footprints of dinosaurs. Interestingly, the footprints were initially attributed to giant birds. They were somewhat similar to tracks made by the largest of the living birds, such as the ostrich and emu.

The first fossilized skeletal remains to be identified as those of giant, extinct reptiles were discovered by miners in western Europe. These first discoveries were initially presumed to be astonishingly gigantic, extinct lizards. However, several naturalists recognized substantial anatomical differences between the fossil bones and those of living reptiles. The first of these finds were bones of a 35- to 50-foot-long (10 to 15 meters) carnivore named *Megalosaurus* and a large herbivore named *Iguanodon*. Fossils of both were found in sedimentary rocks in mines in England, Belgium, and France.

Discoveries of fantastic, extinct oversized reptiles in Europe were soon followed by even more exciting finds of dinosaur fossils in North America and elsewhere. These events captured the fascination of both naturalists and the general public. Museums started to develop extraordinary displays of reassembled dinosaur skeletons.

Dinosaur bones uncovered by archaeologists near Kauchanaburi, Thailand. *(Reproduced by permission of The Stock Market.)*

This initial period of discoveries occurred in the late nineteenth and early twentieth centuries. During this period many of the most important finds were made by North American paleontologists (scientists who study fossils). An intense scientific interest grew over these American discoveries of fossilized bones of gargantuan, seemingly preposterous animals. Unfortunately, the excitement and scientific frenzy led to a rather passionate competition among some paleontologists, who wanted to be known for discovering the biggest, or the fiercest, or the weirdest dinosaurs.

Other famous discoveries of fossilized dinosaur bones have been made in the Gobi Desert of eastern Asia. Some of those finds include nests with eggs that contain fossilized embryos (the earliest stage of development). The embryos have been used to study dinosaur development. Some nests contain hatchlings, suggesting that dinosaur parents cared for their young. In addition, the clustering of the nests of some dinosaurs suggests that the animals had led a social life. They may have nested together, for example, for mutual protection against predatory dinosaurs.

By now, fossilized dinosaur bones have been discovered on all continents. Discoveries of fossils in the high Arctic and in Antarctica suggest that the climate there was much warmer when dinosaurs roamed Earth. It also is likely that polar dinosaurs were migratory, traveling to high latitudes to feed and breed during the summer and returning to lower latitudes during the winter.

Although the most important fossil records of dinosaurs involve their bones, other sorts of evidence exist as well. In addition to footprints, eggs, and nests, imprints of dinosaur skin, feces, rounded gizzard stones, and even possible stomach contents have been found. In early 2000, paleontologists announced they had discovered the fossilized heart of a dinosaur that had died some 66 million years ago. Uncovered in South Dakota, the heart was encased in a natural sarcophagus of stone in the chest cavity of a dinosaur's fossil skeleton.

Fossilized plant remains are sometimes associated with deposits of dinosaur fossils. These finds allow scientists to make inferences as to the habitats of these animals. Inferences also can be based on the geological context of the locations of fossils, for example, their nearness to a marine shore, or geographical position, as is the case of polar dinosaurs. All of these types of information have been studied and used to infer the shape, physiology, behavior, and ecological relationships of extinct dinosaurs.

Major groups of dinosaurs

Scientists have only incomplete knowledge of the way in which dinosaurs were related to each other and to other major groups of reptiles.

The reason for this fact, of course, is that dinosaurs can be studied only through their fossilized remains. These remains are often rare and fragmentary, especially those that are millions or hundreds of millions of years old. Nevertheless, some dinosaur species bear clear resemblances to each other, while also being obviously distinct from certain other dinosaurs.

The dinosaurs evolved from a group of early reptiles known as thecodonts, which arose during the Permian period (290 million to 250 million years ago) and were dominant throughout the Triassic (250 million to 208 million years ago). It appears that two major groups of dinosaurs evolved from the thecodonts, the ornithischian ("bird hips") dinosaurs and the saurischian ("lizard hips") dinosaurs. These two groups are distinguished largely on the basis of the anatomical structure of their pelvic or hip bones. In general, dinosaurs can be classified as carnivorous (meat-eating) or herbivorous (plant-eating).

Carnivorous dinosaurs. The carnosaurs were a group of saurischian predators that grew large and had enormous hind limbs but tiny fore limbs. *Tyrannosaurus rex,* perhaps the best known of all dinosaurs, was once considered the largest carnivore that ever stalked Earth's landscape. Its scientific name is derived from Greek words for "absolute ruler lizard." This fearsome predator reached a maximum length of 40 feet (12 meters), and may have weighed as much as 7 to 9 tons (6.5 to 8 metric tons). *Tyrannosaurus rex* had a massive head and a mouth full of about 60 dagger-shaped, sharp, serrated teeth. Those teeth grew to a length of 6 inches (15 centimeters) and were renewed throughout the life of the animal. This predator probably ran in a lumbering fashion on its powerful hind legs. The hind legs also may have been used as sharp-clawed, kicking weapons. Scientists think that *Tyrannosaurus rex* may have initially attacked its prey with powerful head-butts and then torn the animal apart with its enormous jaws. Alternatively, *Tyrannosaurus rex* may have been primarily a scavenger of dead dinosaurs. The relatively tiny fore legs of *Tyrannosaurus rex* probably only had minor uses. The long and heavy tail of the dinosaur was used as a counterbalance for the animal while it was running and as a stabilizing prop while it was standing.

Tyrannosaurus rex's distinction as the largest carnivore was taken away in 2000 when a team of scientists announced they had discovered the fossilized bones of a previously unknown dinosaur species that had lived about 100 million years ago. The bones of six of the dinosaurs were unearthed in Patagonia, a barren region on the eastern slopes of the Andes Mountains in South America. The scientists estimated that the needle-nosed, razor-toothed, meat-eating giant measured up to 45 feet (14 meters) in length. Like *Tyrannosaurus rex,* it had a tail and short front legs, but it was heavier and had slightly shorter back legs. It also was probably more terrifying than *Tyrannosaurus rex.*

Not all of the dinosaurian predators were enormous. *Deinonychus,* for example, was a dinosaur that grew to about 10 feet (3 meters) and weighed about 220 pounds (100 kilograms). *Deinonychus* was one of the so-called "running lizards." These dinosaurs were fast, agile predators that probably hunted in packs. As a result, *Deinonychus* was probably a fearsome predator of animals much larger than itself. One of *Deinonychus's* hind claws was enlarged into a sharp, sicklelike, slashing weapon. The claw was probably used to slash and tear apart its victim.

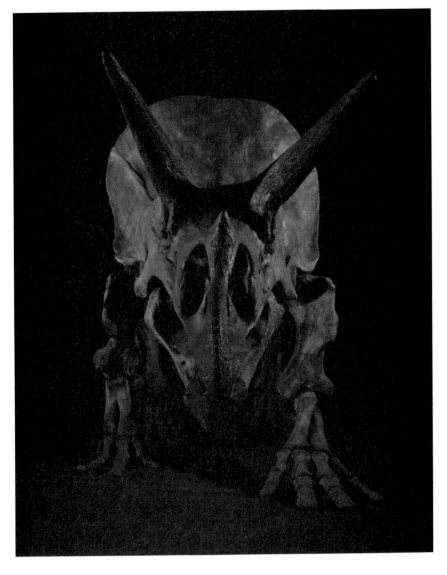

A fossilized skeleton of a *Triceratops,* a gentle, plant-eating ornithischian with three horns on its head. *(Reproduced by permission of Photo Researchers, Inc.)*

The most infamous small carnivorous dinosaur is *Velociraptor,* or "swift plunderer." *Velociraptor* attained a length of about 6 feet (2 meters). Restorations of this fearsome, highly intelligent, pack-hunting "killing machine" were used in the popular movie *Jurassic Park.*

Herbivorous dinosaurs. The sauropods were a group of large saurischian herbivores that included the world's largest-ever terrestrial animals. This group rumbled along on four enormous, pillarlike, roughly equal-sized legs, with a long tail trailing behind. Sauropods also had very long necks, and their heads were relatively small. Their teeth were peglike and were used primarily for grazing rather than for chewing their diet of plant matter. Digestion was probably aided by large stones in an enormous gizzard, in much the same way that modern, seed-eating birds grind their food.

Perhaps the most famous of all sauropods was *Apatosaurus,* previously known as *Brontosaurus.* (The *Apatosaurus* was the first of the two to be discovered, and what was thought to be a different dinosaur, the *Brontosaurus,* was discovered later. In the 1980s it was discovered that they were really the same dinosaur, so they are all now referred to as *Apatosaurus.*) *Apatosaurus* achieved a length of 65 feet (20 meters) and a weight of 30 tons (27 metric tons).

A dinosaur footprint in Tuba City, Arizona. *(Reproduced by permission of JLM Visuals.)*

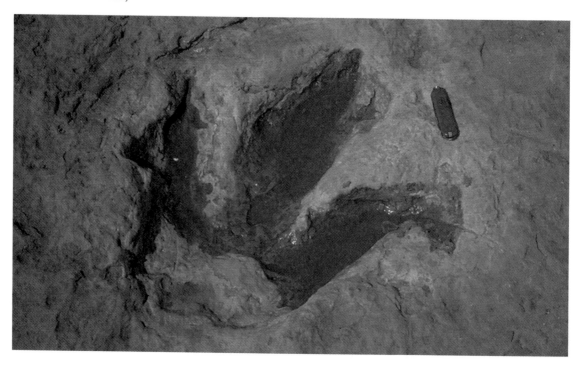

Diplodocus was related to *Brontosaurus,* but had a much longer body. A remarkably complete skeleton of *Diplodocus* has been found that is 90 feet (27 meters) long overall, with a 25-foot (8-meter) neck, a 45-foot (14-meter) tail, and an estimated body weight of 11 tons (10 metric tons). *Brachiosaurus* was an even larger herbivore, with a length as great as 100 feet (30 meters) and an astonishing weight that may have reached 80 tons (73 metric tons).

What became of the dinosaurs?

Many theories have been proposed to explain the extinction of the last of the dinosaurs about 65 million years ago. Some of the more interesting ideas include the intolerance of these animals to rapid climate change, the emergence of new species of plants that were toxic to the herbivorous dinosaurs, an inability to compete successfully with the rapidly evolving mammals, destruction of dinosaur nests and eggs by mammalian predators, and some sort of widespread disease to which dinosaurs were not able to develop immunity. All of these hypotheses are interesting, but the supporting evidence for any of them is not enough to convince most paleontologists that the dinosaurs became extinct for any of these reasons.

Perhaps the most widely accepted theory today is based on the belief that a planet-wide catastrophe resulted in the extinction not only of the dinosaurs but also of hundreds of other species. Scientists have now found evidence that such a catastrophe may have occurred when a large asteroid struck Earth 65 million years ago off the northern tip of the Yucatan Peninsula of Mexico. In such an impact, huge amounts of dust and debris would have been thrown into the atmosphere. Carbonates and sulfate rocks would have also been vaporized, releasing chemicals into the atmosphere that produced sulfur and the greenhouse gas carbon dioxide. The dust and rocks would have blocked out sunlight for an extended period of time, perhaps for years, which would have killed off plants in large numbers. Deprived of plants, choking on carbon dioxide, and suffering showers of caustic sulfuric acid rain, the dinosaurs would have died out.

[*See also* **Evolution; Fossil and fossilization; Geologic time; Paleontology**]

Diode

A diode is an electronic device that has two electrodes (conductors of electrical currents) arranged in such a way that electrons (subatomic particle having a negative charge) can flow in only one direction. Because of this ability to control the flow of electrons, a diode is commonly used as a rectifier—a device that converts alternating current into direct current. (Alternating current is an electric current that flows first in one direction and then in the other. But alternating current fed into a diode can move in one direction only, thereby converting the current to a one-way flow known as a direct current.)

Types of diodes

In general, two types of diodes exist. Older diodes were vacuum tubes containing two metal components, while newer diodes are solid-state devices consisting of one n-type and one p-type semiconductor. (Solid-state devices are electronic devices that take advantage of the special conducting properties of solids. Semiconductors are substances that conduct an electric current but do so very poorly.)

Vacuum tube diode. The working element in a vacuum tube diode is a metal wire or cylinder known as the cathode. Surrounding the cathode or placed at some distance from it is a metal plate. The cathode and plate are sealed inside a glass tube from which all air is removed. The cathode is also attached to a heater which, when turned on, causes the cathode to glow. As the cathode glows, it emits electrons. The diode acts as a rectifier, allowing the flow of electrons in only one direction, from cathode to plate.

Semiconductors. Newer types of diodes are made from n-type semiconductors and p-type semiconductors. N-type semiconductors contain small impurities that provide an excess of electrons with the capability of moving through a system. P-type semiconductors contain small impurities that provide an excess of positively charged "holes" that are capable of moving through the system.

A semiconductor diode is made by joining an n-type semiconductor with a p-type semiconductor through an external circuit containing a source of electrical current. The current is able to flow from the n-semiconductor to the p-semiconductor, but not in the other direction. In this sense, the n-semiconductor corresponds to the cathode and the p-semiconductor to the plate in the vacuum tube diode. The semiconductor diode has most of the same functions as the older vacuum diode, but it operates much more efficiently and takes up much less space than does a vacuum diode.

[*See also* **Cathode; Electrical conductivity; Electric current**]

Dioxin

The term dioxin refers to a large group of organic compounds that are structurally related to benzene (a colorless, flammable, and toxic [poisonous] liquid hydrocarbon, meaning it contains both carbon and hydrogen atoms) and may contain one or more chlorine atoms in their structures. Those compounds that do contain chlorine are known as chlorinated dioxins and are of the greatest environmental interest today.

Production and use

Dioxins have no particular uses. They are not manufactured intentionally but are often formed as by-products of other chemical procedures. Two such processes involve the manufacture of 2,4,5-T (2,4,5-trichlorophenoxyacetic acid) and hexachlorophene. 2,4,5-T was once a popular herbicide (weed-killing agent), while hexachlorophene was an antibacterial agent used in soaps and other cleaning products. The use of both compounds has now been banned in the United States.

Dioxins are also formed as by-products of other industrial operations, such as the incineration of municipal wastes and the bleaching of wood pulp.

Toxicity

All 75 chlorinated dioxins known to science are believed to be toxic to some organisms at one level or another. The most toxic of these compounds is believed to be TCDD, or 2,3,7,8-tetrachlorodibenzo-p-dioxin. The differences in toxicities of the chlorinated dioxins is illustrated by the effects of TCDD on guinea pigs, hamsters, and humans.

The toxicity of a substance is commonly measured by a property known as LD_{50}. LD_{50} stands for "lethal dose—50 percent." That is, the LD_{50} for a substance is the amount of that substance needed to kill one-half of a test population of animals in some given period of time, usually a few days.

The LD_{50} for TCDD for guinea pigs is 0.0006 mg/kg (milligrams per kilogram). That is, adding no more than 0.0006 milligram of TCDD per kilogram of body weight will kill half of any given population of guinea pigs. In contrast, the LD_{50} for hamsters is 0.045 milligrams per kilogram, making them thousands of times more resistant to TCDD than guinea pigs.

The LD_{50} for TCDD for humans cannot be determined the way it is for experimental animals. (Scientists can't just add TCDD to the diet of humans to see how much is needed to kill half the individuals in a sample.) However, researchers do have data about the health effects of TCDD on humans from other sources. The most important of these sources are studies of: (1) industrial exposures to toxins of chemical workers, (2) people living near a toxic waste dump at Times Beach, Missouri, and (3) an accidental release of TCDD at Seveso, Italy, in 1976.

The accident in Italy involved an explosion at a chemical plant that released between 2 to 10 pounds (1 and 5 kilograms) of TCDD to the surroundings. Residues as large as 51 ppm (parts per million) were later detected in environmental samples. This accident caused the deaths of some livestock and 187 cases of chloracne among humans. Chloracne is a skin condition caused by exposure to chlorine or certain of its compounds. But scientific studies failed to find increased rates of disease among those exposed to TCDD or a higher rate of birth defects among the offspring of pregnant women in the population.

Overall, studies suggest that humans are among those animals least affected by TCDD. Chloracne is probably the most common symptom of exposure to TCDD. The data on other health effects, such as disease (primarily cancer), deaths, and birth defects are much less clear. Some scientists argue that—except for massive exposures to the chemical—TCDD should be of little or no concern to health scientists. Other scientists are especially troubled, however, by possible effects resulting from long-term exposures to even small doses of TCDD.

TCDD in Vietnam

Some of the most troubling questions about dioxin concern the use of Agent Orange during the Vietnam War (a civil war between communist North Vietnam and noncommunist South Vietnam, fought mainly in the 1960s and 1970s; the United States began bombing the North in 1964, but U.S. troops were withdrawn in 1973, shortly before the North's victory).

Agent Orange is a 50:50 mixture of 2,4,5-T and a related compound, 2,4-D (2,4-dichlorophenoxyacetic acid). The U.S. military sprayed large quantities of Agent Orange over the Vietnam countryside during the war in order to deprive the Vietnamese of food and cover. According to some estimates, more than 56,000 square miles (1.5 million hectares) of Vietnamese land were sprayed at least once.

Authorities believe that the Agent Orange used in Vietnam was contaminated by TCDD at concentrations averaging about 2 parts per million. If true, a total of 240 to 375 pounds (110 to 170 kilograms) of TCDD was sprayed with herbicides onto Vietnam.

Many veterans of the Vietnam War have claimed that exposure to TCDD caused them serious medical problems. A number of studies have been carried out by both governmental and private organizations, but so far those studies have not provided clear and convincing proof of the veterans' claims. Veterans' groups and other interested citizens, however, continue to push their cases about possible health effects from exposure to Agent Orange and TCDD.

[*See also* **Agrochemicals**]

Disease

Disease can be defined as any change in body processes that impairs its normal ability to function. The human body has certain basic requirements that must be met if it is to function normally. These requirements include the proper amount of oxygen, acidity, salinity, and other conditions. These conditions must all be maintained within a very narrow range. A deviation from that range can cause disease to develop.

Most diseases can be classified into one of three major categories: infectious diseases; noninfectious diseases; and diseases for which no cause has yet been identified. At one time, a number of conditions were also classified as genetic diseases. This category includes conditions such as sickle-cell anemia, phenylketonuria, Tay-Sachs disease, cystic fibrosis, and galactosemia. These conditions are now more appropriately known as genetic disorders.

Infectious diseases

At one time, humans were totally mystified as to the causes of common diseases such as typhoid, typhus, pneumonia, mumps, yellow fever, pneumonia, smallpox, rabies, syphilis, gonorrhea, tuberculosis, and rheumatic fever. Explanations ranged from punishment by God for evil deeds to acts of magicians or witches to an unbalance in the composition of the blood.

During the eighteenth century, the true nature of such diseases was finally discovered. Largely due to the work of the French chemist Louis Pasteur (1822–1895) and the German bacteriologist Robert Koch (1843–1910), scientists learned that infectious diseases were caused by organisms that entered the human body and upset its normal healthy state. In most cases, these organisms were too small to be seen with the unaided eye: bacteria, viruses, and fungi, for example. In other cases, they were caused by various types of worms. Diseases of the latter type are usually called parasitic diseases because the worms live off the human body as parasites.

The human body includes a number of devices to protect itself from infectious diseases. The first in line of these devices is skin. Skin can be thought of as a protective envelope surrounding the body. That envelope generally is able to prevent disease-causing organisms (germs) from entering the body.

One way in which disease can develop is for a break to occur in the skin, as in a cut or scrape. Germs that would normally be prevented from

Smallpox on the arm of a man in India. *(Reproduced by permission of Phototake.)*

entering the body are able to invade the bloodstream through such openings. At that point, the body puts into action a second line of defense: the immune system. The immune system is a complicated collection of chemical reactions that release compounds that attack and destroy invading organisms. Without an immune system, the human body would become ill nearly every time there was a cut in the skin.

In some instances, the immune system is unable to react adequately to an invasion of germs. In such cases, disease develops.

The spread of infectious disease. One characteristic of infectious diseases is that they are easily transmitted from one person to another. For example, a person who has contracted typhus can easily pass that disease to a second person simply by coming into contact with that person. Germs travel from the carrier of the disease to the uninfected person.

Disease can be spread by many methods other than direct contact, such as through water, food, air, and blood. Waterborne transmission occurs through contaminated water, a common means by which cholera, waterborne shigellosis, and leptospirosis are spread. Foodborne poisoning in the form of bacterial contamination may occur when food is improperly cooked, left unrefrigerated, or prepared by an infected food handler.

Diseases such as measles and tuberculosis can be transmitted through the air. Any time an infected person coughs or sneezes, infectious organisms can travel more than 3 feet (0.9 meter) to an uninfected person. Fungal infections such as histoplasmosis, coccidioidomycosis, and blastomycosis can also be spread by airborne transmission as their spores are transported on dust particles.

Vectors are animals that carry germs from one person to another. The most common vectors are insects. These vectors may spread a disease either by mechanical or biological transmission. An example of mechanical transmission occurs when flies transfer the germs for typhoid fever from the feces (stool) of infected people to food eaten by healthy people. Biological transmission occurs when an insect bites a person and takes in infected blood. Once inside the insect, the disease-causing organisms may reproduce in the gut, increasing the number of parasites that can be transmitted to the next person. The disease malaria is spread by the *Anopheles* mosquito vector.

Epidemics. Diseases sometimes spread widely and rapidly through a population. Such events are known as epidemics. One of the best-known epidemics in human history was the Black Death that struck Europe in the mid-fourteenth century. Caused by the microorganism *Pasteurella* *pestis,* the Black Death is also known as the bubonic plague, or simply, plague. Plague is transmitted when fleas carried by squirrels and rats bite humans and transfer the *P. pestis* from one person to another.

Once it reached Europe from Asia in about 1350, the plague was virtually unstoppable. In some areas, whole towns were destroyed as people either died or moved away trying to avoid the disease. Over an eight-year period, an estimated 25 million people died of the disease.

Other examples of epidemics include the worldwide spread of cholera during the mid-nineteenth century, the influenza epidemic in the United States in the early twentieth century, and the HIV (human immunodeficiency virus) epidemic in the United States beginning in the early 1980s.

Protection against infectious diseases. When scientists learned the cause of infectious diseases, they also developed the ability to prevent and cure such diseases. For example, people can now be vaccinated as a protection against many types of infectious disease. A vaccine is a material that can be injected into a person to ward off attacks by certain disease-causing organisms. The material may consist of very weak concentrations of the organism itself or of dead organisms. The presence of these organisms in the bloodstream stimulates the body's immune system to start producing chemicals that will fight off the disease if and when it actually enters the body.

In addition, scientists have discovered and invented a host of substances that will fight the germs that cause infectious diseases. The class of drugs known as antibiotics, for example, can be used to aid the body's natural immune system in combatting disease-causing organisms that have entered the body.

Childhood diseases. Chicken pox, measles, and mumps are all common childhood diseases. The term childhood disease is a bit misleading, however, since any one of these diseases can be contracted by a person at any age. The term developed simply because the diseases are much more common among young children than they are among adults.

The diseases named above are all infectious, caused by a virus. They are generally spread by direct contact between an infected and a noninfected person, and since young children are often in direct contact with each other—on the playground, riding a school bus, or in a classroom—they are especially susceptible to such diseases.

All three viral diseases have a somewhat similar pattern. There is a period of incubation, during which the virus reproduces within a person's body. Obvious symptoms then begin to appear: a rash in the case of chicken pox and measles and inflamed and swollen glands in the case of mumps. All three diseases normally disappear after a period of time, generally without leaving any long-term effects.

Most children can now be protected against childhood diseases by means of a regular program of immunization (vaccinations). There are, as yet, however, few if any treatments for the diseases themselves.

Noninfectious diseases

Vaccinations and drugs have been so successful in treating infectious diseases that they are no longer the massive threat to human health that they once were. Today, the greatest threat to human health are noninfectious diseases such as heart disease, cancer, and diseases of the circulatory system. In some cases, the nature of these diseases is well understood, and medical science is making good progress in combatting

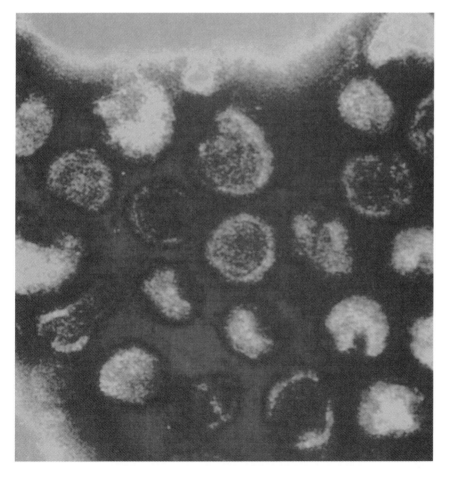

A magnified look at the disease rubella, also called German measles. *(Reproduced by permission of Custom Medical Stock Photo, Inc.)*

Epidemiology

Your town is in a state of panic. Dozens of people have become ill in the past month with a disease that no one can recognize. You and your neighbors are worried that you too will become ill with the disease. To whom can you turn for help?

This puzzle calls for the work of an epidemiologist. An epidemiologist is a scientist who studies the cause and spread of disease. The epidemiologist uses a number of sophisticated techniques in his or her work. One of these techniques is sometimes called source and spread. Interviews are held with people who are ill to find out those with whom they have recently come into contact. The goal is to find out from whom the person got the disease and to whom it might have been passed on. This pattern of disease spread is sometimes called a web of causation.

Epidemiologists also try to track down the agent that caused the disease: a bacterium, virus, fungus, or other organism. They then try to determine how that organism has been transmitted from one person to another. By identifying the specific factors involved in an epidemic, it is sometimes possible to determine preventive actions that can be taken to reduce the occurrence of a disease. For example, it may be that everyone who has come down with the disease in your town has been swimming in the local lake. The disease can be prevented from spreading, then, by warning people not to swim in that lake.

The techniques of epidemiology have also been used to deal with noninfectious diseases. For example, some epidemiologists have argued that gun-related accidents have many of the characteristics of an infectious diseases. They say that people who are injured by guns can be studied in much the same way as people who become ill because of a disease-causing organism. This idea is still relatively new, however, and has yet to prove its worth in dealing with such problems.

them. For example, it is known that a stroke occurs when arteries in the brain become constricted or clogged and are unable to permit the normal flow of blood. The brain is deprived of blood, and cells begin to die, causing loss of muscular control, paralysis, and, eventually, death.

Another noninfectious disease is cancer. The term cancer refers to any condition in which cells in a person's body begin to grow in a rapid and uncontrolled way. The causes of such growth are probably many and varied.

For example, certain types of chemicals (known as carcinogens) can cause cancer. Certain kinds of tars, dyes, and organic compounds are known to be responsible for various forms of cancers. The largest single fatal form of cancer, lung cancer, is caused by chemicals found in tobacco smoke. Exposure to various forms of radiation are also known to cause cancer. People who are exposed to long periods of sunshine are at high risk for the development of various forms of skin cancer, the most dangerous of which is malignant melanoma. Some scientists also believe that some forms of cancer may be caused by viruses (which would make them an infectious disease).

[*See also* **Ebola virus; Genetic disorders; Legionnaires' disease; Plague**]

Distillation

Distillation is a technique by which two or more substances with different boiling points can be separated from each other. For example, fresh water can be obtained from seawater (water that contains salts) by distillation. When seawater is heated, water turns into a vapor that can be condensed and captured. The salts in the seawater remain behind.

General principles

In contrast to the preceding example, distillation is most commonly used to separate two or more liquids from each other. Imagine a mixture of three liquids, A, B, and C. A has a boiling point of 86°F (30°C); B has a boiling point of 104°F (40°C); and C has a boiling point of 122°F (50°C). Ordinary gasoline is such a mixture, except that it consists of many more than three components.

The three-liquid mixture described above is added to a distillation flask, such as the one in the accompanying figure of the distillation setup. The mixture in the flask is heated by a Bunsen burner or some other apparatus. The temperature of the liquid mixture rises until it reaches the boiling point of any one liquid in the flask. In our example, that liquid is A, which boils at 86°F. Liquid A begins to boil when the temperature in the flask reaches 86°F. It turns into a vapor at that temperature, rises in the distilling flask, and passes out of the flask arm into the condenser.

The condenser consists of a long tube surrounded by a larger tube. The outer tube contains water, which enters near the bottom of the condenser and leaves near the top. The water passing through the outer jacket of the condenser cools the vapor passing through the inner tube. The vapor loses heat and condenses (meaning it changes back to a liquid). It flows out of the condenser and into a receiving container—a flask or beaker placed in position to capture the liquid. The liquid (liquid A) is now known as the distillate, or the product of the distillation.

Meanwhile, the temperature in the distilling flask has not changed, as indicated by the thermometer in the mouth of the flask. Heat added to the liquid mixture is used to vaporize liquid A, not to raise the temperature of the mixture. That temperature will begin to rise only when liquid A has completely boiled away. By watching the thermometer, therefore, an observer can know when liquid A has been completely removed from the liquid mixture. At that point, the receiver containing pure liquid A can be removed and replaced by a new receiver.

Once liquid A has boiled away, the temperature in the distilling flask begins to rise again. When it reaches 104°F, liquid B begins to boil away, and the sequence of events observed with liquid A is repeated. Eventually, pure samples of A, B, and C can be collected.

The distillation process described here has been known and used by humans for many centuries. It was used by ancient civilizations to prepare alcoholic beverages such as beer and wine and was perfected by those pre-chemists of the Middle Ages (400–1450) known as alchemists. It has now been refined for use with many kinds of liquids under many different circumstances. For example, some liquids decompose (break apart) at or be-

A typical laboratory distillation setup. *(Reproduced by permission of The Gale Group.)*

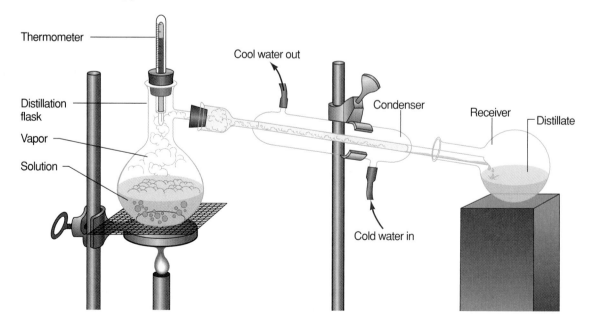

Thermometer

Cool water out

Distillation flask

Condenser

Receiver

Distillate

Vapor

Solution

Cold water in

low their boiling points. Vacuum distillation is used for such liquids. In vacuum distillation, air is pumped out of the distilling flask. Under reduced pressure in the flask, liquids boil away at temperatures less than their boiling points (below the point at which they would otherwise decompose).

Applications

Distillation is among the most important and widely used industrial operations today. About 95 percent of all separation processes today are carried out in industry with more than 40,000 distillation systems. Those systems generally consist of structures that look very different from the one shown in the distillation setup figure. For example, a petroleum refining plant is usually distinguished by a group of distilling towers that rise more than 100 feet (30 meters) into the air. The principle on which such towers operate, though, is no different from the one described above.

In petroleum refineries, crude oil is heated at the bottom of the refining tower. The hundreds of compounds that make up crude oil each boil off at their own characteristic boiling point. They rise in the refining tower, are cooled, and condense to liquids. Collectors at various heights in the tower are used to draw off those liquids into various fractions known by designations such as gasoline, diesel oil, heating oil, and lubricating oil.

A similar process is used in many other chemical processes. It is common that many by-products are produced along with some desired product in a chemical reaction. The desired product can be separated from the by-products by means of distillation.

Doppler effect

The Doppler effect is an effect observed in light and sound waves as they move toward or away from an observer. One simple example of the Doppler effect is the sound of an automobile horn. Picture a person standing on a street corner. A car approaches, blowing its horn. As the car continues moving toward the person, the pitch of the horn appears to increase; its sound goes higher and higher. As the car passes the observer, however, the effect is reversed. The pitch of the car horn becomes lower and lower.

Explanation

All waves can be defined by two related properties: their wavelength and frequency. Wavelength is the distance between two adjacent (next to

▼ Words to Know

Hubble's law: The law that shows how the redshift of a galaxy can be used to determine its distance from Earth.

Redshift: The lengthening of the frequency of light waves as they travel away from an observer; most commonly used to describe movement of stars away from Earth.

each other) and identical parts of the wave, such as between two wave crests (peaks). Frequency is the number of wave crests that pass a given point per second. For reference, the wavelength of visible light is about 400 to 700 nanometers (billionths of a meter), and its frequency is about 4.3 to 7.5×10^{14} hertz (cycles per second). The wavelength of sound waves is about 0.017 to 17 meters, and their frequency is about 20 to 20,000 hertz.

The car horn effect described above was first explained around 1842 by Austrian physicist Johann Christian Doppler (1803–1853). To describe his theory, Doppler used a diagram like the one shown in the accompanying figure of the Doppler effect. As a train approaches a railroad station, it sounds its whistle. The sound waves coming from the train travel outward in all directions. A person riding in the train would hear nothing unusual, just the steady pitch of the whistle's sound. But a person at the train station would hear something very different. As the train moves forward, the sound waves from its whistle move with it. The train is chasing or crowding the sound waves in front of it. An observer at the train station hears more waves per second than someone on the train. More waves per second means a higher frequency and, thus, a higher pitch.

An observer behind the train has just the opposite experience. Sound waves following the train spread out more easily. The second observer detects fewer waves per second, a lower frequency, and, therefore, a lower-pitched sound.

It follows from this explanation that the sound heard by an observer depends on the speed with which the train is traveling. The faster the train is moving in the above example, the more its sound waves are bunched together or spread out—thus, the higher or the lower the pitch observed.

Doppler effect in light waves

Doppler predicted that the effect in sound waves would also occur with light waves. That argument makes sense since sound and light are both transmitted by waves. But Doppler had no way to test his prediction experimentally. Doppler effects in light were not actually observed, in fact, until the late 1860s.

In sound, the Doppler effect is observed as a difference in the pitch of a sound. In light, differences in frequency appear as differences in color. For example, red light has a frequency of about 5×10^{14} hertz; green light, a frequency of about 6×10^{14} hertz; and blue light, a frequency of about 7×10^{14} hertz.

Suppose that a scientist looks at a lamp that produces a very pure green light. Then imagine that the lamp begins to move rapidly away from the observer. The Doppler effect states that the frequency of the light will decrease. Instead of appearing to be a pure green color, it will tend more toward the red end of the spectrum. The faster the lamp moves away from the observer, the more it will appear to be first yellow, then orange, then red. At very high speeds, the light coming from the lamp will no longer look green at all, but will have become red.

Applications

The green lamp example described above has been used to great advantage by astronomers when observing stars. The light of a star as seen

The Doppler effect. *(Reproduced by permission of The Gale Group.)*

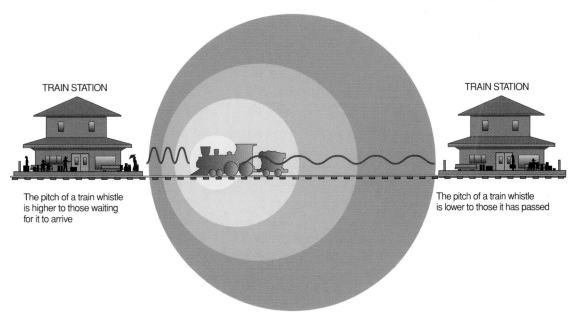

TRAIN STATION

TRAIN STATION

The pitch of a train whistle is higher to those waiting for it to arrive

The pitch of a train whistle is lower to those it has passed

from Earth is always slightly different from its true color because all stars are in motion. When astronomers observe stars in our own Milky Way galaxy, for example, they find that the color of some stars is shifted toward the blue, while the color shift in other stars is toward the red. Blueshift stars are moving toward Earth, and redshift stars are moving away from Earth.

In 1923, American astronomer Edwin Hubble (1889–1953) made an interesting discovery. He found that all stars outside our own galaxy exhibit redshifts of light. That is, all stars outside our galaxy must be moving away from Earth. Furthermore, the farther away the stars are, the more their redshift and, thus, the faster they are moving away from us.

Hubble's discovery is one of the most important in all of modern astronomy. It tells us that the universe as a whole is expanding. Like dots on the surface of a balloon that's being blown up, galaxies throughout the universe are racing away from each other. One conclusion to be drawn from this discovery is that—at some time in the past—all galaxies must have been closer together at the center of the universe. Ever since that time, those galaxies have been moving away from each other. This conclusion is the basis for the currently popular theory about the creation of the universe, the big bang theory.

The Doppler effect has many other practical applications. Weather observers can bounce radar waves off storm clouds. By studying the frequency of the waves that return, they can determine the direction and speed with which the clouds are moving. Similarly, traffic police use radar guns to determine the speed of vehicles. The faster a car or truck is traveling, the greater the change in the frequency of the radar waves it reflects.

Sound waves are used for underwater observations. A submarine sends out sound waves that are reflected off other underwater objects, such as another submarine or a school of fish. The frequency of the reflected sound tells the direction and speed of the other object.

[*See also* **Radar; Redshift; Sonar; Wave motion**]

Drift net

Drift nets are free-floating nets used in oceans to snare fish by their gills. Each net can measure up to 50 feet (15 meters) deep and 55 miles (89 kilometers) long. Because drift nets are not selective, many fish and marine mammals are trapped in them. Those unwanted by fishermen, such as sharks, turtles, seabirds, and dolphins, are removed from the nets and thrown back, dead, into the ocean. Drift nets are an extraordinarily de-structive fishing technology.

Ecological damage caused by drift nets

Drift nets are used in all of the world's major fishing regions, and the snaring of unintended marine species is always a serious problem. This is especially true in the commercial fishing of swordfish, tuna, squid, and salmon. During the late 1980s, drift nets were estimated to have killed as many as one million dolphins and porpoises annually. In addition, millions of seabirds, tens of thousands of seals, thousands of sea turtles, and untold numbers of sharks and other large species of fish were accidentally snared and killed.

Great lengths of drift nets and other fishing nets are lost at sea every year, especially during severe storms. Because the nets are made of materials that do not degrade or break down easily, they continue to snare fish and marine mammals underwater for many years. It is unknown how many are killed as a result of these so-called "ghost nets."

In response to mounting concerns about the harmful nature of drift nets, the United Nations banned the use of those nets longer than 1.5 miles (2.5 kilometers) in 1993. Although this regulation would not eliminate

A striped dolphin caught in a French drift net off the Azores in the North Atlantic Ocean. (*Reproduced by permission of Greenpeace Photos.*)

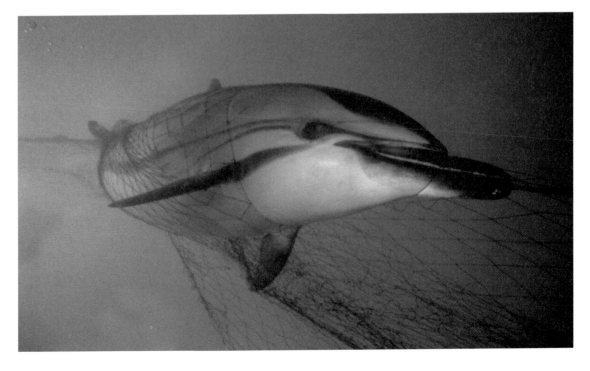

the snaring of unintended species, it would reduce the amount killed by as much as two-thirds. Unfortunately, there has been a great deal of resistance from the fishing industry and fishing nations to this regulation. Many fisheries continue to use much longer nets.

Drought

Drought is an extended period of exceptionally low precipitation. A drought can feature additional weather characteristics, including high temperatures and high winds.

Although low precipitation (rain, snow, or sleet) marks both droughts and deserts, the two are different. A desert is a region that experiences low precipitation as an everyday occurrence. A drought, on the other hand, is a temporary condition in which precipitation is abnormally low for a particular region. Droughts may occur at any time in any part of the world and last anywhere from days to weeks to decades.

The U.S. National Weather Service recognizes three categories of drought. A dry spell occurs when there is less than .03 inch (.08 centimeter) of rainfall during a minimum of 15 consecutive days. A partial drought occurs when the average daily rainfall does not exceed .008 inch (.02 centimeter) during a 29-day period. An absolute drought occurs when there is no measurable rainfall over a period of at least 15 days.

The intensity of a drought may be measured by the ability of living things in the affected area to tolerate the dry conditions. Some plants quickly fall prey to droughts while others, such as cacti and mesquite trees, survive dry conditions by either storing water in their tissues or by going dormant (a state in which growth activity stops). Although a drought may end abruptly with the return of adequate rainfall, the effects of a drought on the landscape and its inhabitants may last for years.

History

Droughts have taken place around the world throughout history. Some scientist theorize that droughts brought about the migrations of early humans. From 1876 to 1879, severe droughts in China caused the deaths of millions of people from lack of food. In 1921, a drought along the Volga River basin in Russia led to the deaths of almost five million people, more than the total number of deaths in World War I (1914–18).

The best-known American drought occurred on the Great Plains region during the mid-1930s. Labeled the Dust Bowl, the affected area covered almost 50 million acres in parts of Colorado, New Mexico, Kansas, Texas, and Oklahoma. During this period, dust storms destroyed crops and buried agricultural fields with drifting sand and dust. As depicted by American writer John Steinbeck in his award-winning novel *The Grapes of Wrath,* many farm families had to abandon their land.

Drought and famine have severely affected areas throughout Africa. Beginning in the late 1960s, in the Sahel region south of the Sahara Desert in northern Africa, a prolonged drought contributed to the deaths of an estimated 100,000 people. The region was struck again by drought in the mid-1980s and early 1990s. War and drought in Ethiopia in the early 1980s brought about the starvation of an estimate one million people and the forced migration of hundreds of thousands of others.

Drought combined with social unrest continued to afflict many countries at the beginning of the twenty-first century. The African nations of Djibouti, Eritrea, Ethiopia, Kenya, Somalia, and Sudan were all hit hard by a massive drought that began in the late 1990s. Conflicts like the

A dust storm approaching Springfield, Colorado, that would engulf the city in total darkness for almost an hour. Dust storms can occur when soil not securely anchored by vegetation is dried out by drought then blown up by winds. *(Reproduced courtesy of the Library of Congress.)*

border war between Eritrea and Ethiopia slowed the delivery of famine aid. Devastating civil wars also worsened the effect of drought in the countries of Afghanistan and Tajikistan. The unrelenting droughts were the worst those countries had seen in decades.

The El Niño weather phenomenon typically brings about droughts in various parts of the world as it disrupts normal weather patterns. Perhaps one of the worst such droughts occurred in Southeast Asia as a result of the 1997–98 El Niño period. The monsoon rains that normally drench the area each September were delayed. Consequently, the jungle fires set by farmers to clear land were not damped by the usual rain, but instead raged out of control, propelled by hot winds. The smoke from the fires hung over Southeast Asia like a thick, dirty blanket. It quickly became the worst pollution crisis in world history. At least 1,000 people died from breathing the toxic air; several hundred thousand more were sickened.

Human impact on droughts

Soil that lacks humus (nutrient-rich material resulting from decaying plants) and the binding property of plant roots cannot absorb or retain moisture properly. Dry, crusty soil is easily moved by winds. The overgrazing of farm animals, the overcultivation of farmland, and the clear-cutting of forests all contribute to such soil conditions, adding to the severity of droughts.

[See also **Erosion; Hydrologic cycle**]

DVD technology

DVD stands for digital versatile disc, although it is also commonly referred to as digital video disc, due to the popularity of DVDs in the video industry. DVD technology allows for the storage of a large amount of data using digital technology. DVDs can store up to 17 gigabytes, compared to the storage capacity of a compact disc (CD), which is approximately 680 megabytes (1 gigabyte is equal to 1,024 megabytes).

Construction of a DVD

A DVD is a thin, circular wafer of clear plastic and metal measuring 4.75 inches (12 centimeters) in diameter with a small hole in its center. In its most basic form, a DVD is one 0.02-inch-thick (0.06-centimeter-thick) disc; at its greatest capacity, a DVD is two such discs, compressed together to create a double-sided disc 0.04 inch (0.12 centimeter) thick.

The digital data (the binary language of ones and zeroes common to all computers) used in DVDs is encoded onto a master disc. This disc is then used to create copies of itself. A laser (a device used to create a narrow, intense beam of very bright light) burns small holes, called pits, into a microscopic layer of metal, usually aluminum. These pits correspond to the binary ones; smooth areas of the disc untouched by the laser, called land, correspond to the binary zeroes. Once the pits have been burned, the metal is coated with a protective, transparent layer.

Origin of the DVD

DVD technology originated in the early 1990s after movie companies saw how successful the digital medium of CDs was to the music consumer. The music industry had seen the CD virtually replace the popular long-playing (LP) vinyl record, a nondigital and, therefore, lower-quality medium. On the motion picture side, the dominant medium of choice for the home consumer was the VHS (video home system) tape, also a nondigital medium. In an attempt to develop a product that would result in improved visual and audio quality, movie companies worked on various digital video formats for the home consumer. The result was the development of the DVD.

By the mid-1990s, such entertainment giants as Time-Warner and Sony agreed that it was in the entertainment industry's best interest to work together as a group. By 1996, this new group helped create a standard for digitized movies and, thereby, promote the new high-quality technology. Introduced to the market in March 1997, DVD has become the most popular electronics consumer item to date.

DVD benefits

In contrast to a VHS videotape, a DVD provides better visual and audio quality. In the case of a motion picture, for instance, a DVD provides much sharper images than a VHS videotape due to the use of MPEG-2 compression. (MPEG stands for Moving Pictures Experts Group, an organization of people that meets several times a year to establish standards for audio and video encoding. The term "MPEG," however, has become a nickname for the technology itself. Compression refers to the process of condensing various audio and video signals into less space while improving the quality.)

A DVD also has great storage capacity. In addition to being able to store an entire movie itself, a DVD can also hold a number of additional features as well: these include alternate endings, audio and subtitles in different languages, cast biographies, deleted scenes, documentary footage on how the film was made, and a variety of camera angles, as well as the capacity for surround sound (four microphones, four amplifiers, and four loudspeakers that together provide remarkably realistic sound reproduction though appropriate sound equipment is needed). Additionally, a two-layered DVD allows a movie to be presented in both the more square-shaped television screen size as well as the more rectangular-shaped theater screen size, commonly called letterbox (so-called because its rectangular image resembles a mailbox or letterbox).

DVD and computers

Although DVD is most popularly thought of as a movie-viewing medium, its ability to enhance the computer industry is incredible. DVD-ROM (read-only memory) drives hook up to a computer and read DVDs. This allows a consumer to watch movies and play games with enhanced graphics on a computer. Four variations of DVD-ROMs have the ability to record data: DVD-R (recordable) can be rewritten only once; DVD-RAM (random access memory) and DVD-RW and DVD+RW (two types of rewritable discs) can be rewritten thousands of times. The three types of rewritable discs have compatibility differences and also vary in the amount of information they can contain. All three are in competition with each other.

The future of DVD technology

As of the beginning of the twenty-first century, DVD technology had yet to significantly impact videocassette recorder (VCR) sales, due primarily to the lack of standards for DVD recording technology and the expensive prices of DVD recorders. Because different manufacturers are offering their own recording technology, market forces have yet to determine which technology will lead the way. Currently, the music industry is studying the viability of DVDs as a consumer-friendly media option.

[*See also* **Compact disc; Video recording**]

Dyes and pigments

Dyes and pigments are substances that impart color to a material. The term colorant is often used for both dyes (also called dyestuffs) and pigments.

The major difference between dyes and pigments is solubility (the tendency to dissolve in a liquid, especially water). Dyes are usually soluble—or can be made to be soluble—in water. Once a dye is dissolved in water, the material to be dyed can be immersed in the dye solution. As the material soaks up the dye and dries, it develops a color. If the material then retains that color after being washed, the dye is said to be colorfast.

Pigments are generally not soluble in water, oil, or other common solvents. To be applied to a material, they are first ground into a fine powder and thoroughly mixed with some liquid, called the dispersing agent or vehicle. The pigment-dispersing agent mixture is then spread on the material to be colored. As the dispersing agent dries out, the pigment is held in place on the material.

In most cases, dyes are used for coloring textiles, paper, and other substances, while pigments are used for coloring paints, inks, cosmetics, and plastics.

History

Many dyes can be obtained from natural sources, such as plants, animals, and minerals. In fact, humans have known about and used natural dyes since the dawn of civilization. Red iron oxide, for example, has long been used to color cloth and pottery and to decorate the human body. Today, T-shirts dyed with naturally occurring red dirt (iron oxide) are popular among tourists on Hawaii's island of Kauai. Red dirt imparts a brilliant orangish-red color to cloth that is almost impossible to wash out. Other natural dyes include sepia, obtained from cuttlefish, and Indian yellow, obtained from the urine of cows that have been force-fed mango leaves.

Some natural dyes are expensive to produce, difficult to obtain, or hard to use. Royal purple got its name because it comes only from the tropical murex snail. So many snails were needed to produce even the smallest amount of dye that only royalty could afford to use it. The dye known as indigo, obtained from the *Indigofera* plant, imparts a beautiful blue color to material, but it is insoluble in water. It must first be converted to a different (reduced) chemical form that is yellow and is soluble in water. In that form, the indigo can be used for dyeing. Once attached to a material and exposed to air, the yellow form of indigo is converted back (oxidized) to its original blue form.

A revolution in colorant history occurred in 1856, when English chemist William Henry Perkin (1838–1907) discovered a way to manufacture a dye in the laboratory. That dye, mauve, was produced from materials found in common coal tar. Perkin's discovery showed chemists that dyes and pigments could be produced synthetically (by humans in a lab). It was no longer necessary to search out natural products for use as colorants.

Today, the vast majority of dyes and pigments are produced synthetically. These products are easier and less expensive to make than are natural products. In addition, their colors are more consistent from batch to batch than the various samples of natural colorants.

Applications

Dyes can be applied to materials in a variety of ways. The simplest approach is to dissolve the dye in water and then immerse the material within the dye solution. A person who accidentally stains an item of clothing by spilling red wine on it has actually dyed it, although probably not as intended. Any dye that attaches itself to a material in this way is called a direct dye. The dye sticks to the material by forming chemical bonds that survive even after washing.

Whether a dye will attach itself directly to a material or not depends on the chemical nature of both the dye and the material being dyed. Some compounds will dye silk but not wool, or cotton but not polyester. Any

Fabric dye. *(Reproduced by permission of The Stock Market.)*

dyeing process, therefore, involves finding materials to which any given colored compound will attach itself.

Mordant dyeing involves the use of a chemical that combines with the dye to form an insoluble compound (meaning it cannot be dissolved). Suppose dye B will not stick directly to fabric A. In order to color fabric A with dye B, a third material—the mordant (M)—will have to be introduced. M will adhere (stick) to both A and B.

In the mordant process, the mordant is first applied to the fabric. After the mordant has dried, the dye is added. The dye sticks to the mordant, and the fabric is able to take on the color of the dye, forming an insoluble bond.

Pigments

Pigments are applied to a surface as a mixture that always consists of at least two parts (the pigment itself and the vehicle) and usually many more components. For example, a thinner such as turpentine is often added to a given mixture to make it easier to apply. One of the simplest paints that you imagine, then, might consist of red iron oxide, linseed oil (the vehicle), and turpentine (the thinner).

The purpose of the vehicle in this mixture is to carry the pigment onto the surface, much as motor vehicles carry people and goods. A thinner is often needed because many vehicles are thick, viscous (sticky) materials that are difficult to apply with a brush.

After the pigment/vehicle/thinner mixture has been applied to a surface, two changes occur. First, the thinner evaporates leaving the pigment/vehicle mixture evenly spread on the surface. Next, the vehicle slowly undergoes a chemical change (oxidation) that converts it from a thick liquid to a solid. Since the pigment particles are trapped in the hardened vehicle, a thin, tough skin of colored material becomes attached to the surface.

Utilization

Nearly every industry uses colorants in one way or another. About 7,000 different dyes and pigments exist and new ones are patented every year. Dyes are used extensively in the textile (fabric used in clothing) industry and paper industry. Leather and wood are colored with dyes. Food is often colored with natural dyes or with synthetic dyes that have been approved by a federal agency (proven safe for human consumption). Petroleum-based products such as waxes, lubricating oils, polishes, and gasoline are colored with dyes. Dyes are also used to stain biological samples, fur, and hair. And special dyes are added to photographic emulsions for color photographs. Plastics, resins, and rubber products are usually colored by pigments.

Dyslexia

Dyslexia is a learning disorder characterized by difficulty reading and writing. Dyslexia is not caused by poverty, psychological problems, lack of education, or laziness. People who are identified as dyslexic generally have normal or above-normal intelligence, normal eyesight, and tend to come from average families. It is not unusual for a student with dyslexia to fail English while earning straight As in science.

There are dozens of symptoms associated with the disorder. Dyslexic people may skip words, reverse the order of letters in a word (writing or reading "was" for "saw"), or drop some letters from a word (reading "run" instead of "running"). They may invent strange spellings for common words, have difficulty remembering and following sequences (like reciting the alphabet in order), and have cramped, illegible handwriting.

A student with dyslexia has difficulty copying words. (Reproduced by permission of Photo Researchers, Inc.)

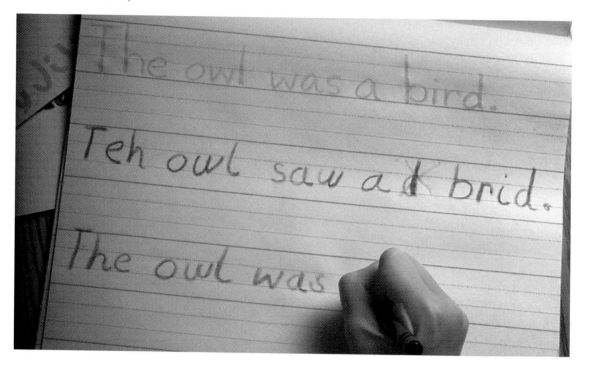

Causes of dyslexia

Scientists generally agree that dyslexia results from a neurological problem in the areas of the brain involved in reading. Several regions of the brain—all located in the brain's left side—have been identified as controlling the complicated task of reading and writing. What part of the reading task is processed in each area is not yet clear. Even more mysterious is how the brain translates abstract symbols like printed letters into ideas.

In normal reading, the eye sends pictures of abstract symbols to the brain. Each symbol is then transferred along different routes to various portions of the brain for interpretation. Scientists suspect that in a dyslexic person, something jams the transfer of that information.

Scientists generally agree that genetics plays a role in dyslexia. Studies of twins show that if one twin is dyslexic, the other is likely to have the disorder. Other studies show that the disorder, which affects about 8 percent of the population, tends to run in families. It is common for a child with dyslexia to have a parent or other close relative with the disorder. Because 90 percent of dyslexic people are male, scientists are investigating the relationship of male hormones to the disorder.

Treating dyslexia

Those with mild cases of dyslexia sometimes learn to compensate on their own. Many reach remarkable levels of achievement. Italian artist, scientist, and engineer Leonardo da Vinci (1452–1519) is thought to have been dyslexic. It is also believed that German-born American physicist Albert Einstein (1879–1955) was dyslexic.

Early diagnosis and prompt treatment seem to be the keys to overcoming the challenges of dyslexia. Linguistic (language) and reading specialists can help those with the disorder learn how to develop and apply reading and writing skills.

Ear

The human ear is the organ responsible for hearing and balance. The ear consists of three parts: the outer, middle, and inner ears.

Outer ear

The outer ear collects external sounds and funnels them through the auditory system. The outer ear is composed of three parts, the pinna (or auricle), the auditory canal, and the eardrum (tympanic membrane).

What are commonly called ears—the two flaplike structures on either side of the head—are actually the pinnas of the outer ear. Pinnas are skin-covered cartilage, not bone, and are therefore flexible.

The auditory canal is a passageway that begins at the ear and extends inward and slightly upwards. In the adult human it is lined with skin and hairs and is approximately 1 inch (2.5 centimeters) long. The outer one-third of the canal is lined with wax-producing cells and fine hairs. The purpose of the ear wax and hairs is to protect the eardrum (which lies at the end of the canal) by trapping dirt and foreign bodies and keeping the canal moist.

The eardrum is a thin, concave membrane stretched across the inner end of the auditory canal much like the skin covering the top of a drum. The eardrum marks the border between the outer ear and middle ear. In the adult human, the eardrum has a total area of approximately 0.1 square inch (0.6 square centimeter). The middle point of the eardrum—called the umbo—is attached to the stirrup, the first of three bones contained within the middle ear.

Words to Know

Auditory canal: Tunnel or passageway that begins at the external ear and extends inward toward the eardrum.

Cochlea: Snail-like structure in the inner ear that contains the anatomical structures responsible for hearing.

Eardrum: Also known as the tympanic membrane, a thin membrane located at the end of the auditory canal separating the outer ear from the middle ear.

Eustachian tube: A passageway leading from the middle ear to the throat.

Organ of Corti: Structure located in the cochlea that is the chief part of the ear through which sound is perceived.

Ossicles: Three tiny, connected bones located in the middle ear.

Otitis media: Ear infection common in children in which the middle ear space fills with fluid.

Otosclerosis: Hereditary disease that causes the ossicles to stiffen due to a build up of calcium.

Pinna: Also called auricle or external ear, the flaplike organ on either side of the head.

Vestibular system: System within the body that is responsible for balance and equilibrium.

Middle ear

The middle ear transmits sound from the outer ear to the inner ear. The middle ear consists of an oval, air-filled space approximately 0.1 cubic inch (2 cubic centimeters) in volume. Contained in this space are three tiny bones called ossicles (pronounced OS-si-kuls). Because of their shapes, the three ossicles are known as the hammer (malleus), the anvil (incus), and the stirrup (stapes).

Connecting the middle ear to the throat is the eustachian tube (pronounced you-STAY-she-an). This tube is normally closed, opening only as a result of muscle movement during yawning, sneezing, or swallowing. The eustachian tube causes air pressure in the middle ear to match the air pressure in the outer ear. The most noticeable example of eustachian tube function occurs when there is a quick change in altitude, such as when a plane takes off. Prior to takeoff, the pressure in the outer ear is equal to the pressure in the middle ear. When the plane gains altitude, the air pressure in the outer ear decreases, while the pressure in the middle ear remains the same, causing the ear to feel "plugged." In response to this the ear may "pop." The popping sensation is actually the quick opening and closing of the eustachian tube, and the equalization of pressure between the outer and middle ear.

Inner ear

The inner ear is responsible for interpreting and transmitting sound and balance sensations to the brain. The inner ear is small (about the size of a pea) and complex in shape. With its series of winding interconnected chambers, it has been called a labyrinth. The main components of the inner ear are the vestibule, semicircular canals, and the cochlea (pronounced COCK-lee-a).

The vestibule, a round open space, is the central structure within the inner ear. The vestibule contains two membranous sacs—the utriculus (pronounced you-TRIK-yuh-les) and the sacculus (pronounced SAC-yuh-les). These sacs, lined with tiny hairs and attached to nerve fibers, function as a person's chief organs of balance.

Attached to the vestibule are three loop-shaped, fluid-filled tubes called the semicircular canals. These canals, arranged perpendicular to each other, are a key part of the vestibular system. Two of the canals help the body maintain balance when it is moving vertically, such as in falling and jumping. The third maintains horizontal balance, as when the head or body rotates.

The cochlea is the organ of hearing. The cochlea consists of a bony, snail-like shell that contains three separate fluid-filled ducts or canals. The middle canal contains the basilar membrane, which holds the organ of Corti, named after Italian anatomist Alfonso Giacomo Gaspare Corti (1822–1876) who discovered it. The organ contains some 20,000 hair cells connected at their base to the auditory nerve. The organ is the site where sound waves are converted into nerve impulses, which are then sent to the brain along the auditory nerve.

Hearing

Sound vibrations travel through air, water, or solids in the form of sound waves. These waves are captured by the pinna of the outer ear and transmitted through the auditory canal to the eardrum.

The anatomy of the human ear. *(Reproduced by permission of The Gale Group.)*

The eardrum vibrates in response to the pressure of the sound waves. The initial vibration causes the eardrum to be pushed inward by an amount equal to the intensity of the sound, so that loud sounds push the eardrum inward more than soft sounds. Once the eardrum is pushed inward, the pressure within the middle ear causes the eardrum to be pulled outward, setting up a back-and-forth motion.

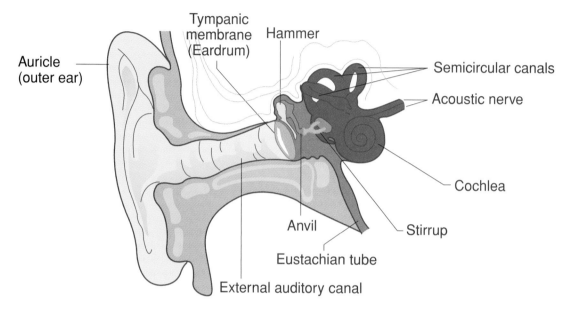

Outer ear

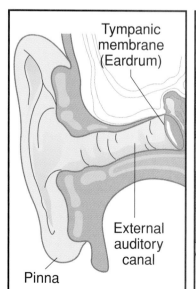

Middle ear

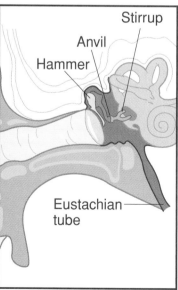

Inner ear

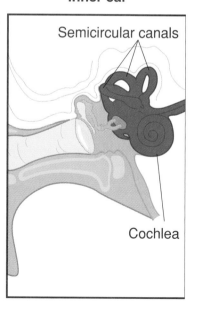

The movement of the eardrum sets all three ossicles in motion. The vibrating pressure of the stirrup (last ossicle) on the small opening leading to the inner ear sets the fluid in the cochlea in motion. The fluid motion causes a corresponding, but not equal, wavelike motion of the basilar membrane.

When the basilar membrane moves, it causes the small hairs on the top of the hair cells of the Corti to bend. The bending of the hair cells causes chemical actions within the cells themselves, creating electrical impulses in the nerve fibers attached to the bottom of the hair cells. The nerve impulses travel up the auditory nerve to the brain. Loud sounds cause a large number of hair cells to be moved and many nerve impulses to be transmitted to the brain.

Hearing disorders

A problem in any part of the ear may cause a hearing disorder or hearing loss. In general, hearing loss may be caused by a birth defect, an injury, or a disease.

Birth defects may include missing pinnas, low-set pinnas, abnormalities in the size and shape of the pinnas, or a narrowing or complete closure of the auditory canal. These conditions may be corrected by surgery. Other birth defects that can affect hearing include premature birth, low birth weight, and illnesses suffered by the mother during pregnancy (such as measles). These defects damage the inner ear, specifically the cochlea. Medical treatment for this type of hearing loss is very rare. However, many individuals gain some benefit by wearing hearing aids.

Injury to the eardrum is common. A perforated or torn eardrum may be caused by a buildup of fluid in the middle ear, a direct puncture, explosion, or blast. When the normally taut eardrum is perforated, it becomes slack and does not vibrate properly. In some cases, the eardrum will heal itself without treatment. In more serious cases, surgical treatment may be necessary.

Ossicles are very susceptible to trauma. Injured ossicles may become unattached, broken, or excessively stiff. Once again, surgical treatment may correct the disorder and restore hearing.

There are a variety of diseases that can affect the ear, causing a hearing loss. Otitis media, a common condition in children, refers to an ear infection within the middle ear space. When this normally air-filled space is filled with fluid, the movement of the bones is affected and sound cannot be transmitted easily. The typical treatment for otitis media is medication (antibiotics and decongestants). Otosclerosis is a disease that causes the ossicles to stiffen due to a build-up of calcium. It is a hereditary disorder (inherited through family), develops in early adulthood, and is more common in women than men. Treatment may include surgery or the use of a hearing aid.

Earth

Earth, the third planet from the Sun, is our home planet. Its surface is mostly water (about 70 percent) and it has a moderately dense nitrogen-and-oxygen atmosphere that supports life—the only known life in the universe. From space, Earth appears as a shining blue ball with white swirling clouds covering vast oceans and irregular-shaped landmasses that are varying shades of green, yellow, brown, and white.

Earth orbits the Sun at a distance of about 93,000,000 miles (150,000,000 kilometers), taking 365.25 days to complete one elliptical (oval-shaped) revolution. The planet rotates once about its axis almost every 24 hours. It is not truly spherical, but bulges slightly at its equator. Earth's diameter at the equator is roughly 7,926 miles (12,760 kilometers), while its diameter at the poles is 7,900 miles (12,720 kilometers). The circumference of Earth at its equator is about 24,830 miles (40,000 kilometers).

Earth's only natural satellite, the Moon, orbits the planet at an average distance of about 240,000 miles (385,000 kilometers). Some scientists believe that Earth and the Moon should properly be considered a double planet, since the Moon is larger relative to our planet than the moons of most other planets.

Unlike the outer planets, which are composed mainly of light gases, Earth is made of heavy elements such as iron and nickel, and is therefore much denser. Hot at first due to the collisions that formed it about 4.5 million years ago, Earth began to cool. Its components began to separate themselves according to their density. Heavy abundant elements, iron and nickel, formed Earth's core. Outside the core numerous elements were compressed into a dense but pliable (bendable) substance called the mantle. Finally, a thin shell of cool, silicon-rich rock formed at Earth's surface, called the crust or lithosphere. Formation of the crust from the initial molten blob took half a billion years.

Earth's atmosphere

Earth's atmosphere is the only planetary atmosphere in the solar system capable of sustaining life. It is made of 78 percent nitrogen, 21 percent oxygen, and a 1 percent mixture of gases dominated by argon.

Various theories have been proposed as to the origin of these gases. One theory states that when Earth was formed, the gases were trapped in layers of rock beneath the surface. They eventually escaped, primarily through volcanic eruptions, to form the atmosphere. Water vapor was the most plentiful substance spewed out, and condensed (change from a gas to a liquid) to form the oceans. Carbon dioxide was second in terms of quantity, but most of it dissolved in the ocean waters or was altered chemically through reactions with other substances in the rocks. Nitrogen came out in smaller amounts, but always remained in its present form because it never underwent reactions or condensation. It is believed that for that reason, nitrogen is the most abundant gas in the atmosphere today.

Oxygen only became a part of Earth's atmosphere when green plants came into being. Through the process called photosynthesis, green plants convert carbon dioxide into oxygen. Oxygen is also removed from the atmosphere when green plants, as well as animals, die. As they decay, they oxidize, a process that uses up oxygen.

The coastlines of Africa, Antarctica, and Arabia are visible in this photo of Earth taken in December 1972 by Apollo 17. *(Reproduced by permission of National Aeronautics and Space Administration.)*

Another more recent theory regarding the development of Earth's atmosphere states that the elements found in it were deposited there by comets. Debris from comets has been shown to have carbon and nitrogen in roughly the same proportion as the atmosphere. During its early development, Earth was the site of repeated comet collisions.

Ninety-nine percent of the atmosphere's mass is contained in the first 40 to 50 miles (65 to 80 kilometers) above Earth's surface. This relatively thin atmosphere insulates the planet by allowing the Sun's visible light to pass through the atmosphere and warm the surface. The resulting

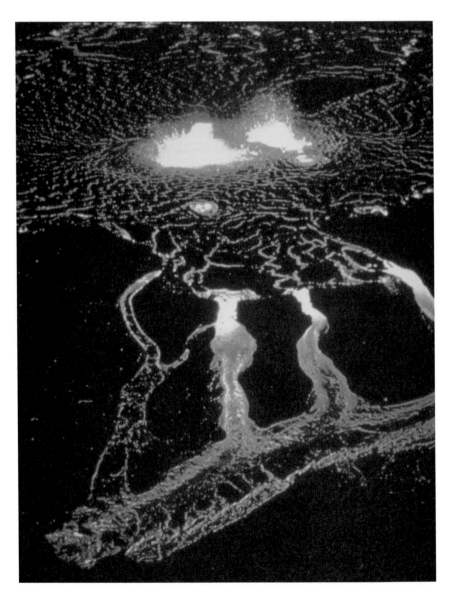

Molten lava from the Hawaiian volcano Kilauea. *(Reproduced by permission of JLM Visuals.)*

heat (infrared radiation) is reradiated from the surface, but is prevented from totally escaping back into space by carbon dioxide, methane, and water vapor in the atmosphere. These so-called greenhouse gases absorb most of this energy and re-emit back to the surface, keeping the planet at relatively stable, warm temperatures. The average surface temperature is 59°F (15°C).

While keeping in necessary heat radiation, components in the atmosphere block dangerous forms of radiation from reaching the surface. These include X rays and ultraviolet radiation, which is absorbed by the ozone layer located at about 15 miles (24 kilometers) above Earth's surface.

Earth's surface

The surface of Earth is divided into dry landmasses and oceans. Landmasses occupy roughly 57.5 million square miles (148.9 million square kilometers) of the planet's surface, while oceans cover roughly 139.5 million square miles (361.3 square kilometers).

Landmasses are in a constant, though slow, state of change. They move, collide, and break apart according to a process called plate tectonics. The lithosphere is not one huge shell of rock; it is composed of several large pieces called plates. These pieces are constantly in motion, because Earth's interior is dynamic, with its core still molten (liquid) and with large-scale convective (circulating) currents in the upper mantle. This resulting giant furnace beneath the surface moves land no more than a few centimeters a year, but this is enough to have profound consequences. The unending cycle of mountain building (caused by movement of the crustal plates) and erosion (by wind and water) has formed every part of Earth's surface today.

Earth is mostly covered with water. The mighty Pacific Ocean covers nearly half of the globe. The existence of oceans implies that there are large areas of the lithosphere that are lower than others, which form huge basins. Early in the planet's history these basins filled with water condensing (raining) out of the primordial (primitive) atmosphere. Additional water was brought to Earth by impacting comets, whose nuclei were made of water and ice.

The atmosphere has large circulation patterns, and so do the oceans. Massive streams of warm and cold water flow through them. Circulation patterns in the oceans and in the atmosphere are driven by temperature differences between adjacent areas and by the rotation of Earth, which helps create circular flows. Oceans play a critical role in the overall weather patterns of our planet. Storms are ultimately generated by moisture in the atmosphere, and evaporation from the oceans is the prime source of such moisture. Oceans respond less dramatically to changes in solar energy than land does, so the temperature over a given patch of ocean is far more stable than one on land.

Life

The presence of life on Earth is, as far as we know, unique. The origin of life on Earth is not fully understood, but scientists believe amino acids, the essential building blocks of life, formed in the primordial oceans billions of years ago. Over eons, these building blocks combined and evolved into higher and higher life-forms.

Life has existed on dry land only for the most recent 10 percent of Earth's history, since about 385 million years ago. Once life got a foothold beyond the oceans, however, it spread rapidly. Within 200 million years, forests spread across the continents and the first amphibians evolved into dinosaurs. Mammals became dominant after the demise of the dinosaurs 65 million years ago. Only in the last 2 million years, that is, 0.05 percent of Earth's history, have humans appeared.

[*See also* **Africa; Asia; Antarctica; Atmosphere, composition and structure; Australia; Cartography; Earthquake; Earth science; Earth's interior; Europe; Geologic time; Geology; Hydrologic cycle; Moon; North America; Ocean; Paleontology; Plate tectonics; South America; Solar system; Sun; Volcano; Weather**]

Earthquake

An earthquake is an unpredictable event in which masses of rock shift below Earth's surface, releasing enormous amounts of energy and sending out shock waves that sometimes cause the ground to shake dramatically. Not all earthquakes are enormous, but they can become one of Earth's most destructive forces.

Causes of earthquakes

Earth's crust is composed of many huge, rocky plates known as tectonic plates. These plates constantly move slowly across the surface of Earth, bumping into each other, overrunning each other, and pulling away from each other. When the strain produced by these movements increases beyond a certain level, the pent-up energy ruptures the crust and creates

Words to Know

Epicenter: The location where the seismic waves of an earthquake first appear on the surface, usually almost directly above the focus.

Fault: A crack running through rock that is the result of tectonic forces.

Focus: The underground location of the seismic event that causes an earthquake.

Modified Mercalli scale: A scale used to compare earthquakes based on the effects they cause.

Richter scale: A scale used to compare earthquakes based on the energy released by the earthquake.

Seismic waves: Classified as body waves or surface waves, vibrations in rock and soil that transfer the force of the earthquake from the focus into the surrounding area.

a fracture known as a fault. The released pressure also causes the ground-shaking vibrations associated with an earthquake.

The motion of earthquakes: Seismic waves

The vibrations transmitting the shock of an earthquake are called seismic waves (pronounced SIZE-mik). These waves travel outward in all directions, like ripples from a stone dropped in a pond. The area where energy is first released to cause an earthquake is called the focus. The focus lies underground at a shallow, intermediate, or deep depth—down to about 430 miles (700 kilometers). The epicenter is the point on Earth's surface directly above the focus.

Seismic waves travel both through Earth and along its surface. Waves traveling through Earth are called body waves. The two main types are P waves (primary) and S waves (secondary). P waves stretch and compress the rock in their path through Earth. The fastest waves, they move at about 4 miles (6.4 kilometers) per second. S waves move the rock in their path up and down and side to side. They move at about 2 miles (3.2 kilometers) per second.

Seismic waves traveling along Earth's surface are called surface waves or L waves (long). The two main types, Rayleigh waves and Love

Tsunami

A tsunami is a giant wave created by an underwater earthquake, volcano, or landslide. As part of the seabed (ocean floor) rises or drops, water is displaced or moved, producing a great wave. A tsunami (Japanese for "harbor wave") crosses the deep ocean at speeds up to 500 miles (800 kilometers) per hour, but it is only detectable on the surface as a low swell (a wave with no crest). As the giant wave approaches the shallows near shore, it slows down and rises up dramatically, often as much as 200 feet (60 meters). It then strikes the shore with unstoppable force. A wall of water forms when a large tsunami enters straight into a shallow bay or estuary, and can move upriver for many miles.

waves, are named after two prominent seismologists (scientists who study earthquakes). Although surface waves move slower than body waves—less than 2 miles (3.2 kilometers) per second—they cause greater damage. Rayleigh waves cause the ground surface in their path to ripple with little waves. Love waves move in a zigzag along the ground. Both Rayleigh and Love waves set off avalanches, landslides, and other earthquake damage.

Measuring earthquakes

An earthquake's power can be measured in two ways: by intensity (strength) and magnitude (ground covered). While intensity of an earthquake is usually described through people's perceptions and the amount of property destroyed, magnitude is measured by using seismographs or devices that detect ground movement.

Intensity can be measured using the modified Mercalli scale. First developed by Italian seismologist Guiseppe Mercalli (1850–1914) in 1902, the scale compares the surface effects of earthquakes to each other. It is divided into 12 levels, from level 1 meaning "felt by few" to level 12 meaning "total damage."

Magnitude is measured using the Richter scale, developed by American seismologist Charles F. Richter (1900–1985) in 1935. The Richter scale compares the energy released by an earthquake to the energy released by other earthquakes. Each whole number increase in value on the

Opposite Page: A portion of the Hanshin Expressway is twisted down on its side in Nishinomiya after a powerful earthquake rocked the western Japanese city on January 17, 1995. The highway runs from Osaka to Kobe, a port city. Thousands were injured and 1,300 killed. *(Reproduced by permission of AP/Wide World Photos.)*

scale indicates a 10-fold increase in the energy released and a 30-fold increase in ground motion. Therefore, an earthquake of 6 on the Richter scale is 10 times more powerful than an earthquake with a value of 5, which is 10 times more powerful than an earthquake with a value of 4. An earthquake that measures 8 or above on the Richter scale causes total damage.

Earthquake occurrence and prediction

Earth experiences more than one million earthquakes a year. The vast majority of these measure 3.4 or below on the Richter scale and cannot be felt by people. The planet never ceases to vibrate with the motion of its tectonic forces. Full of heat and kinetic energy (the energy of an object due to its motion), Earth has been resounding with the violence of earthquakes for more than four billion years. In recorded human history, great earthquakes have been responsible for some of the most horrendous natural disasters. In the past 800 years, 17 earthquakes have each caused 50,000 or more deaths.

At the beginning of the twenty-first century, an estimated 100 million Americans live on or near an active earthquake fault. Hundreds of millions more lived on or near such faults around the world. Knowing

A National Guardsman walks past all that remains of an apartment house after an earthquake. *(Reproduced by permission of Corbis-Bettmann.)*

the exact time and place an earthquake will occur still lies beyond the ability of scientists. However, in order to interpret seismic activity and possibly to prevent needless deaths, seismologists constantly monitor the stresses within Earth's crust. Ultrasensitive instruments placed across faults at the surface measure the slow, almost imperceptible movement of plates. Other instruments measure phenomena that seem to precede earthquakes. These include changes in tide and ground-water levels, fluctuations in the magnetic properties of rocks, and the swelling or tilting of the ground. Peculiar animal behavior has also been reported before many earthquakes, and scientific research into this phenomenon has been conducted.

[*See also* **Fault; Plate tectonics**]

Earth science

Earth science is the study of the physical components of Earth—its water, land, and air—and the processes that influence them. Earth science can be thought of as the study of the five physical spheres of Earth: atmosphere (gases), lithosphere (rock), pedosphere (soil and sediment), hydrosphere (liquid water), and cryosphere (ice).

Earth scientists, then, must consider interactions between all three states of matter—solid, liquid, and gas—when performing investigations. The subdisciplines of Earth science are many, and include the geosciences, oceanography, and the atmospheric sciences.

The geosciences involve studies of the solid part of Earth and include geology, geochemistry, and geophysics. Geology is the study of Earth materials and processes. Geochemistry examines the composition and interaction of Earth's chemical components. Geophysicists study the dynamics of Earth and the nature of interactions between its physical components.

Oceanography is the study of all aspects of the oceans: chemistry, water movements, depth, topography, etc.

The atmospheric sciences, meteorology and climatology, involve the study of Earth's weather. Meteorology is the study of the physics and chemistry of the atmosphere. One of the primary goals of meteorology is the analysis and prediction of short-term weather patterns. Climatology is the study of long-term weather patterns, including their causes and variations.

To better understand the highly involved and interrelated systems of Earth, scientists from these different subdisciplines often must work together. Today, Earth science research focuses on solving the many problems posed by increasing human populations, decreasing natural resources, and inevitable natural hazards. Computer and satellite technologies are increasingly used in this research.

[*See also* **Earth; Geology; Oceanography; Weather**]

Earth's interior

The distance from Earth's surface to its center is about 3,975 miles (6,395 kilometers). Scientists have divided the interior of Earth into various layers, based on their composition. The crust, or outer portion, varies in depth from 5 to 25 miles (8 to 40 kilometers). Below the crust is the mantle, which extends to a depth of about 1,800 miles (2,900 kilometers). Below that is the core, composed of a liquid outer core about 1,380 miles (2,200 kilometers) in depth, and a solid inner core about 780 miles (1,300 kilometers) deep.

From direct observation, core samples, and drilling projects, scientists have been able to study the rock layers near the planet's surface. However, this knowledge is limited. The deepest drill hole, just over 9 miles (15 kilometers) in depth, penetrates only about 0.2 percent of the distance to Earth's center.

Geologists collect information about Earth's remote interior from several different sources. Some rocks found at Earth's surface originate deep in Earth's crust and mantle. Meteorites that fall to the planet are also believed to be representative of the rocks of Earth's mantle and core. Meteor fragments presumably came from the interior of shattered extraterrestrial bodies within our solar system. It is likely that the composition of the core of our own planet is very similar to the composition of these extraterrestrial travelers.

Another source of information, while more indirect, is perhaps more important. That source is seismic, or earthquake, waves. When an earthquake occurs anywhere on Earth, seismic waves travel outward from the earthquake's center. The speed, motion, and direction of seismic waves changes dramatically as they travel though different mediums (areas called transition zones). Scientists make various assumptions about the composition of Earth's layers through careful analysis of seismic data, a method called subsurface detection.

Words to Know

Asthenosphere: Portion of the mantle beneath the lithosphere composed of partially melted material.

Core-mantle boundary (CMB): Also referred to as the Gutenberg discontinuity, the seismic transition zone separating the mantle from the underlying outer core.

Gutenberg low velocity zone: Seismic transition zone between the lithosphere and the underlying asthenosphere.

Lithosphere: Rigid uppermost section of Earth's mantle combined with the crust.

Mohorovičič discontinuity: Seismic transition zone that marks the transition from the crust to the uppermost section of the mantle.

Seismic transition zone: Interval within Earth's interior where seismic waves, or earthquake waves, display a change in speed and shape.

Seismic waves: Vibrations in Earth's interior caused by earthquakes.

The crust

The crust, the thin shell of rock that covers Earth, contains all the mountains, valleys, oceans, and plains that make up the surface of the planet. There are two types of crust: the continental crust (which underlies Earth's continents) and the oceanic crust (which underlies Earth's oceans). The lighter-colored continental crust is thicker—yet lighter in weight—than the darker-colored oceanic crust. The crust is composed largely of minerals containing the elements calcium, aluminum, magnesium, iron, silicon, sodium, potassium, and oxygen.

The base of the crust (both the oceanic and continental varieties) is determined by a distinct seismic transition zone called the Mohorovičič discontinuity, commonly referred to as the Moho. First discovered in 1909 by the Croatian geophysicist Andrija Mohorovičič (1857–1936), this boundary marks the point where seismic waves pick up speed as they travel through Earth's interior. Since seismic waves travel faster through denser material, Mohorovičič reasoned that there was an abrupt transition from the rocky material in Earth's crust to denser rocks below. The Moho is a relatively narrow transition zone, estimated to be somewhere between 0.1 to 1.9 miles (0.2 to 3 kilometers) thick.

The mantle

Underlying the crust is the mantle, which is composed mainly of minerals containing magnesium, iron, silicon, and oxygen. The uppermost section of the mantle is a rigid layer. Combined with the overlying solid crust, this section is called the lithosphere, which is derived from the Greek word *lithos,* meaning "stone."

At the base of the lithosphere, a depth of about 40 miles (65 kilometers), there is another distinct seismic transition called the Gutenberg low velocity zone. At this level, all seismic waves appear to be absorbed more strongly than elsewhere within Earth. Scientists interpret this to mean that the layer below the lithosphere is a zone of partially melted material. This "soft" zone is called the asthenosphere, from the Greek word *asthenes,* meaning "weak." It extends to a depth of about 155 miles (250 kilometers).

This transition zone between the lithosphere and the asthenosphere is named after American geologist Beno Gutenberg (1889–1960). At the

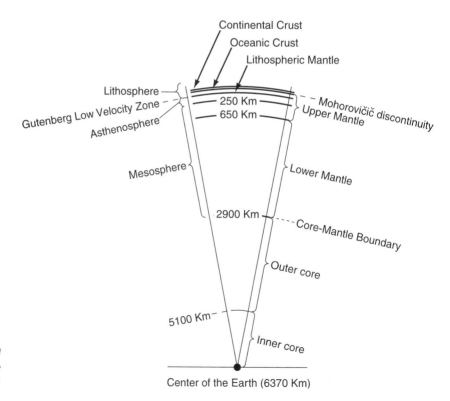

Earth's interior. *(Reproduced by permission of The Gale Group.)*

Gutenberg low velocity zone, the lithosphere is carried "piggyback" on top of the weaker, less rigid asthenosphere, which seems to be in continual motion. This motion creates stress in the rigid rock layers above it, and the slabs or plates of the lithosphere are forced to jostle against each other, much like ice cubes floating in a bowl of swirling water. This motion of the lithospheric plates is known as plate tectonics, and it is responsible for earthquakes, certain types of volcanic activity, and continental drift.

The core

At a depth of 1,800 miles (2,900 kilometers) there is another abrupt change in the seismic wave patterns. This level is known as the core-mantle boundary (CMB) or the Gutenberg discontinuity. At this level, certain seismic waves disappear completely, an indication that the material below is liquid. Accompanying this change is an abrupt temperature increase of 1,300°F (700°C). This hot, liquid outer core is thought to consist mainly of iron. Electric currents in the outer core's iron-rich fluids are believed to be responsible for Earth's magnetic field.

Within Earth's core, at about a depth of 3,200 miles (5,150 kilometers), the remaining seismic waves that passed through the outer liquid core speed up. This indicates that the material in the inner core is solid. The change from liquid to solid in the core is probably due to the immense pressures present at this depth. Based on the composition of meteorite fragments that fell to Earth, scientists believe the inner core to be composed of iron plus a small amount of nickel.

[*See also* **Earthquake; Plate tectonics**]

Eating disorders

Eating disorders are psychological conditions that involve either overeating, voluntary starvation, or both. The best-known eating disorders are probably anorexia nervosa, anorexic bulimia, and obesity. Researchers are not sure what causes eating disorders, although many believe that family relationships, biochemical (physical) abnormalities, and society's preoccupation with thinness all may contribute to their onset.

Eating disorders are virtually unknown in parts of the world where food is scarce. They also are rarely seen in less prosperous groups in developed countries. Although these disorders have been documented throughout history, they have gained attention in recent years. This attention has come, at least in part, because some famous people have died as a result of their eating disorders.

Young people are more likely than older people to develop an eating disorder. The condition usually begins before the age of 20. Although both men and women can develop the problem, it is more common in women. Only about 5 percent of people with eating disorders are male. In either males or females, eating disorders are considered serious and potentially deadly health problems. Many large hospitals and psychiatric clinics have programs designed especially to treat these conditions.

Anorexia nervosa

The word anorexia comes from the Greek adjective *anorektos,* which means "without appetite." But the problem for people with anorexia is not that they aren't hungry. They starve themselves out of fear of gaining weight, even when they are severely underweight. The anorectic's self-image is so distorted that he or she sees himself or herself as "fat" even when that person looks almost like a skeleton. Some anorectics refuse to eat at all; others nibble only small portions of fruit and vegetables or live on diet drinks. In addition to fasting, anorectics may exercise strenuously to keep their weight abnormally low. No matter how much weight they lose, they always worry about getting fat.

This self-imposed starvation takes a heavy toll on the body. Skin becomes dry and flaky. Muscles begin to waste away. Bones stop growing and may become brittle. The heart weakens. With no body fat for insulation, the anorectic has difficulty staying warm. Downy hair starts to grow on the face, back, and arms in response to lower body temperature. In women, menstruation stops and permanent infertility may result. Muscle cramps, dizziness, fatigue, even brain damage and kidney and heart failure are possible. An estimated 10 to 20 percent of people with anorexia die, either as a direct result of starvation or by suicide.

Researchers believe that anorexia is caused by a combination of biological, psychological, and social factors. They are still trying to pinpoint the biological factors, but they have discovered some psychological and social triggers of the disorder. Many people with anorexia come from families in which parents are overprotective and have unrealistically high expectations of their children. Also, the condition seems to run in families, which leads researchers to believe it may have a genetic basis. Anorexia often seems to develop after a young person goes through some stressful experience, such as moving to a new town, changing schools, or going through puberty. Low self-esteem, fear of losing control, and fear of growing up are common characteristics of anorectics. The need for approval, combined with American culture's idealization of extreme thinness, also are believed to contribute to the disorder.

The obvious cure for anorexia is eating. But that is typically the last thing a person with anorexia wants to do. It is unusual for the person himself or herself to seek treatment. More commonly, a friend, family member, or teacher initiates the process. Hospitalization, combined with psychotherapy and family counseling, is often needed to control the condition. Force-feeding may be necessary if the person's life is in danger. About 70 percent of anorexia patients who are treated for about six months

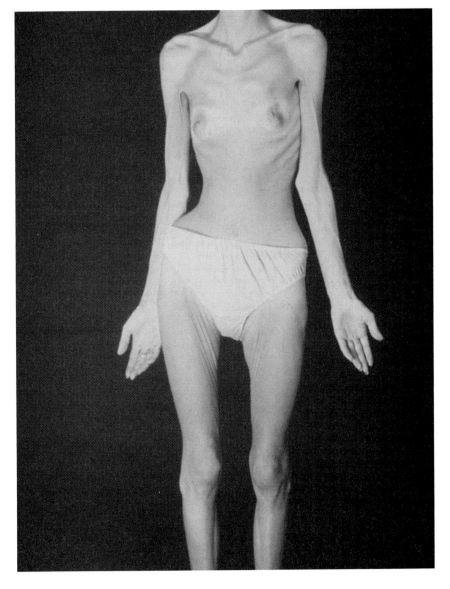

A woman suffering from anorexia nervosa. *(Reproduced by permission of Photo Researchers, Inc.)*

Words to Know

Binge-eating: Unrestrained eating.

Euphoria: A feeling of elation.

Laxative: A chemical that is designed to relieve constipation, often used by bulimics to rid the body of digested food.

Morbid: Having the tendency to produce disorder or disease.

Pinch test: A method of estimating the percent of fat in a person's body by grabbing a small area of skin between the fingers.

Risk factor: Any habit or condition that makes a person more susceptible to a disease.

Serotonin: A naturally occurring chemical that affects nerve transmissions in the brain and influences a person's moods, among other emotions.

return to normal body weight. About 15 to 20 percent can be expected to relapse, however.

Anorexic bulimia

Anorexic bulimia gets its name from the Greek term *boulimos,* meaning "great hunger," or, literally, "the hunger of an ox." The condition is commonly known simply as bulimia. People with bulimia go on eating binges, often gorging on junk food and then forcing their bodies to get rid of the food, either by making themselves vomit or by taking large amounts of laxatives.

Like anorexia, bulimia results in starvation. But there are behavioral, physical, and psychological differences between the two conditions. Bulimia is much more difficult to detect because people who have the disorder tend to be of normal weight or may even be overweight. They tend to hide their habit of binge eating followed by purging by vomiting or using laxatives. In fact, bulimia was not widely recognized, even among medical and mental health professionals, until the 1980s.

Unlike anorectics, bulimics are aware that their eating patterns are abnormal, and they often feel remorse after a binge. For them, overeating offers an irresistible escape from stress. Many suffer from depression, repressed anger, anxiety, and low self-esteem, combined with a tendency toward perfectionism. About 20 percent of bulimics also have problems with alcohol or drug addiction, and they are more likely than nonbulimics to commit suicide.

Many people overeat from time to time but are not considered bulimic. According to the American Psychiatric Association's definition, a bulimic binges on enormous amounts of food at least twice a week for three months or more.

Bulimics plan their binges carefully, setting aside specific times and places to carry out their secret habit. They may go from restaurant to restaurant, to avoid being seen eating too often in any one place. Or they may pretend to be shopping for a large dinner party, when actually they intend to eat all the food themselves. Because of the expense of consuming so much food, some resort to shoplifting.

During an eating binge, bulimics favor high-carbohydrate foods, such as donuts, candy, ice cream, soft drinks, cookies, cereal, cake, popcorn, and bread, consuming many times the amount of calories they normally would consume in one day. No matter what their normal eating habits, they tend to eat quickly and messily during a binge, stuffing the food in their mouths and gulping it down, sometimes without even tasting it. Some bulimics say they get a feeling of euphoria during binges, similar to the "runner's high" that some people get from exercise.

The self-induced vomiting that often follows eating binges can cause all sorts of physical problems, such as damage to the stomach and esophagus, chronic heartburn, burst blood vessels in the eyes, throat irritation, and erosion of tooth enamel from the acid in vomit. Excessive use of laxatives can be hazardous, too. Muscle cramps, stomach pains, digestive problems, dehydration, and even poisoning may result. Over time, bulimia causes vitamin deficiencies and imbalances of critical body fluids, which in turn can lead to seizures and kidney failure.

Some researchers believe that bulimia, as well as other types of compulsive behavior, is related to an imbalance in the brain chemical serotonin. The production of serotonin, which influences mood, is affected by both antidepressant drugs and certain foods. But most research on bulimia focuses on its psychological roots.

Bulimia is not as likely as anorexia to reach life-threatening stages, so hospitalization usually is not necessary. Treatment generally involves psychotherapy and sometimes the use of antidepressant drugs. Unlike anorectics, bulimics usually admit they have a problem and want help overcoming it. Estimates of the rates of recovery from bulimia vary widely, with some studies showing low rates of improvement and others suggesting that treatment usually is effective. Even after apparently successful treatment, however, some bulimics relapse.

Obesity

A third type of eating disorder is obesity. Obesity is caused by excessive overeating. Being slightly overweight is not a serious health risk. But being severely over one's recommended body weight can lead to many health problems.

Doctors do not entirely agree about the definition of obesity. Some experts classify a person as obese whose weight is 20 percent or more over the recommended weight for his or her height. But other doctors say standard height and weight charts are misleading. They maintain that the proportion of fat to muscle, measured by the skinfold pinch test, is a better measure of obesity.

The causes of obesity are complex and not fully understood. While compulsive overeating certainly can lead to obesity, it is not clear that all obesity results from overindulging. Recent research increasingly points to biological, as well as psychological and environmental, factors that influence obesity.

In the United States, people with low incomes are more likely to be obese than are the wealthy. Women are almost twice as likely as men to have the problem, but both men and women tend to gain weight as they age.

In those people whose obesity stems from compulsive eating, psychological factors seem to play a large role. Some studies suggest that obese people are much more likely than others to eat in response to stress, loneliness, or depression. As they are growing up, some people learn to associate food with love, acceptance, and a feeling of belonging. If they feel rejected and unhappy later in life, they may use food to comfort themselves.

Just as emotional pain can lead to obesity, obesity can lead to psychological scars. From childhood on, many obese people are taunted and shunned. They may even face discrimination in school and on the job. The low self-esteem and sense of isolation that typically result may contribute to the person's eating disorder, setting up an endless cycle of overeating, gaining more weight, feeling even more worthless and isolated, then gorging again to console oneself.

People whose obesity endangers their health are said to be morbidly obese. Obesity is a risk factor in diabetes, high blood pressure, arteriosclerosis (hardened arteries), angina pectoris (chest pains due to inadequate blood flow to the heart), varicose veins, cirrhosis of the liver, and kidney disease. Obesity can cause complications during pregnancy and in surgical procedures. Obese people are about one-and-one-half times more likely to have heart attacks than are other people. Overall, the death rate among people ages 20 to 64 is 50 percent higher for the obese than for people of normal weight.

Since compulsive eating patterns often have their beginnings in childhood, they are difficult to break. Some obese people get caught up in a cycle of binging and dieting—sometimes called yo-yo dieting—that never results in permanent weight loss. Research has shown that strict dieting itself may contribute to compulsive eating. Going without favorite foods for long periods makes people feel deprived. They are more likely, then, to reward themselves by binging when they go off the diet. Other research shows that dieting slows the dieter's metabolism. When the person goes off the diet, he or she gains weight more easily.

The most successful programs for dealing with overeating teach people to eat more sensibly and to increase their physical activity (exercise) to lose weight gradually without going on extreme diets. Support groups and therapy can help people deal with the psychological aspects of obesity.

Ebola virus

The Ebola (pronounced ee-BO-luh) virus is the common name for a severe, often-fatal bleeding or hemorrhagic (pronounced hem-or-RAD-jik) fever that first appeared in 1976. It is caused by a new kind of virus called a filovirus (pronounced FY-low-vye-russ) that kills most of its victims with frightening speed. The source of the virus is unknown and there is no cure.

A deadly disease

As a viral hemorrhagic fever, the Ebola virus infects its host and causes sudden fever, muscle aches, and weakness followed by vomiting, diarrhea, breathing and kidney problems, shock, internal and external bleeding, and usually death. It is one of the most deadly disease-causing agents known, and is classified as a Level 4 pathogen (pronounced PATH-o-jen). For comparison, the disease known as AIDS (acquired immuno-deficiency syndrome) is only a Level 2 pathogen. This new disease is par-

Words to Know

Filovirus: A family of lethal thread-shaped viruses that includes Ebola and Marburg.

Virus: A package of chemicals that are far smaller than the living cells they infect. Viruses are not classified as living organisms, since they cannot grow and reproduce on their own, but rely on a host cell to make copies of themselves.

ticularly horrible and has been described by one author as a "molecular shark" that can turn "virtually every part of the body into a digested slime of virus particles." This means that the victim's internal organs break down, with blood oozing eventually from every part of the body.

First outbreak

The first time the new, thread-shaped filovirus was ever seen was in 1967 in Germany and Yugoslavia. In both those countries, research laboratory workers became violently and desperately ill. Seven of thirty-one workers died. All had one thing in common: they had been exposed to the tissues and blood of several African green monkeys. Doctors soon examined the victims's blood and discovered a virus resembling a tangled rope that was unlike any virus they had ever seen. Following this incident, which gave the name Marburg virus to the new microorganism, there were a few cases in the African countries of Zimbabwe, South Africa, and Kenya.

However, in the summer of 1976, a new version of the filovirus appeared in two major outbreaks that occurred almost at the same time. The first of these emerged in the country of Sudan, and the other in the country of Zaire (now known as the Democratic Republic of the Congo), some 500 miles (800 kilometers) away. In both places it was as if a deadly biological bomb had gone off, with hundreds of people becoming ill and dying at a terrible rate. These large outbreaks resulted in more than 550 cases and 340 deaths. Examination of the virus showed that it was similar to the Marburg virus, but not the same. In fact, it was even deadlier. It came to be called the Ebola virus, named after the river in Zaire where it was first recognized.

Four sub-types

Since that first outbreak in 1976, four subtypes or versions of the Ebola virus have been identified so far. The first three, called Ebola-Zaire, Ebola-Sudan, and Ebola-Ivory Coast, are known to have caused disease in humans. The fourth, called Ebola-Reston after the Reston, Virginia, primate laboratory where it was first discovered, seems to only be transmitted by monkeys to monkeys, although it may be the only one of the four viruses that is airborne (meaning it can be spread through particles floating in the air).

Ebola symptoms

People can get the first three Ebola fevers through direct contact with a sick person. This usually happens to hospital workers or family members who are caring for a severely ill victim and who somehow become infected by coming in contact with the victim's blood or other body fluids. In very poor countries, people often are infected when needles are reused instead of thrown away. Within a few days of being infected, most new victims experience a high fever, headache, muscle and stomach pain, fatigue, and diarrhea. Within one week of being infected, most patients experience chest pain, shock, bleeding, and death. Researchers have no explanation for why some people are able to recover from this devastating illness.

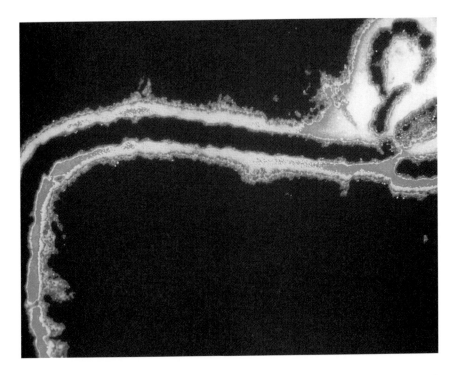

Ebola virus. *(Reproduced by permission of Custom Medical Stock Photo, Inc.)*

Treatment

There is currently no standard treatment for the Ebola virus that results in anything more than making the patient comfortable. The one standard therapy in use is to make sure that patients receive enough proper fluids, as well as maintaining their blood pressure and providing a good supply of oxygen. In hospitals, Ebola patients receive what are called barrier nursing techniques, meaning that they are isolated from other patients and only are tended to by workers who wear protective clothing, masks, gloves, gowns, and goggles. Complete sterilization procedures are also strictly followed.

Although the filovirus family has been known since 1967, scientists still have no idea where the virus lives in nature. So far, every case has been a secondary one, meaning that it was caused by contact from another. Nor do we know the exact mechanism the virus uses to enter the host cell. No drug is known that will work against the virus, nor is there any immunization (pronounced im-mew-nih-ZAY-shun) technique available to protect someone from exposure. No vaccines (pronounced vax-SEENZ) have yet been developed. During the late 1990s and into the new millennium, minor outbreaks had been reported with some regularity in different parts of Africa.

Although there is a great deal to learn about this terrible new disease, we do know that Ebola viruses are found only in Central Africa. Although the source in nature is not yet known, it appears that monkeys are susceptible to infection. The very deadliness of the disease has so far worked against any really massive health disaster because it kills its victims so quickly that they do not have a great chance to infect many others. In some ways, the virus burns itself out before it can spread to a major population center. No case of Ebola fever has ever been reported in the United States.

[See also **Disease**]

Echolocation

In the animal kingdom, certain animals determine the location of an object by producing sounds, then interpreting the echoes that are created when those sounds bounce off the object. This process is called echolocation. The only animals that use this unique sense ability are certain mammals—bats, dolphins, porpoises, and toothed whales. It now is be-

Words to Know

Decibel: A unit used to measure the loudness of sounds.

Frequency: For a sound wave, the number of waves that pass a given point in a particular amount of time.

Mammal: Warm-blooded animals that have a backbone and hair or fur. The female mammal has mammary glands that produce milk to feed her young.

Predator: An animal that hunts, kills, and eats other animals.

lieved that these animals use sound to "see" objects in equal or greater detail than humans.

Mammals developed echolocation as an evolutionary response to night life or to life in dark, cloudy waters. Long ago, bats that ate insects during the day might have been defeated in the struggle for survival by birds, which are better flyers and extremely sharp-sighted. Similarly, toothed whales, porpoises, and dolphins might have been quickly driven to extinction by sharks, which have a very keen sense of smell. These marine mammals not only compete with sharks for food sources, but have themselves been preyed upon by sharks. Echolocation helps them find food and escape from predators.

A golden-capped fruit bat. Bats use echolocation to "see" in the dark. *(Reproduced by permission of Daniel Heuclin, BIOS.)*

Bats

Echolocation in bats was first clearly described by scientists in 1945. Bats that eat frogs, fish, and insects use echolocation to find their prey in total or near-total darkness. After emitting a sound, these bats can tell the distance, direction, size, surface texture, and material of an object from information in the returning echo. Although the sounds emitted by bats are at high frequencies that are out of the range of human hearing, these sounds are very loud—as high as 100 decibels, which is as loud as a chainsaw or jackhammer. People may hear the calls as clicks or chirps. The fruit-eating and nectar-loving bats do not use echolocation. These daytime and early evening bats have strong eyes and noses for finding food.

One question that had puzzled scientists is how a bat can hear the echo of one sound while it is emitting another sound; why is the bat not deafened or distracted by its own sounds? The answer is that the bat is deafened, but only for a moment. Every time a bat lets out a call, part of its middle ear moves, preventing sounds from being heard. Once the bat's call is made, this structure moves back, allowing the bat to hear the echo from the previous call.

Marine mammals

Echolocation may work better underwater than it does on land because it is easier for sound waves to travel through water than through air. Echolocation may even be more effective for detecting objects underwater than light-based vision is on land. Sound with a broad frequency range interacts in a more complex manner with an object it strikes than does light. For this reason, sound can convey more information than light.

Like bats, marine mammals such as whales, porpoises, and dolphins emit pulses of sounds and listen for the echo. Also like bats, these sea mammals use sounds of many frequencies and a highly direction-sensitive sense of hearing to navigate and feed. Echolocation provides all of these mammals with a highly detailed, three-dimensional image of their environment.

Whales, dolphins, and porpoises all have a weak sense of vision and of smell, and all use echolocation in a similar way. The mammal first emits a sound pulse. A large fatty deposit found in its head, sometimes called a melon, helps the mammal to focus the sound. An echo is received at a part of the lower jaw sometimes called the acoustic window. The echo's vibration is then transmitted through a fatty organ in the middle ear where it is converted into a nerve impulse that delivers the information to the brain. The brains of these sea mammals are at least as large relative to their body size as is a human brain to the size of the human body.

Captive porpoises have shown that they can locate tiny objects and thin wires and distinguish between objects made of different metals and of different sizes. This is because an object's material, structure, and texture all affect the nature of the echo returning to the porpoise.

[See also **Acoustics; Cetaceans; Radar; Sonar**]

Eclipse

An eclipse refers to the complete or partial blocking of a celestial body by another body and can be used to describe a wide range of phenomena. Solar and lunar eclipses occur any time the Sun, the Moon, and Earth are all positioned in a straight line. This is an uncommon occurrence because the plane of Earth's orbit around the Sun is different than that of the plane of the Moon's orbit around Earth. Thus, the Moon is usually located just above or below the imaginary plane of Earth's orbit.

Although the Sun is 400 times larger the Moon, the Moon is 400 times closer to Earth. Thus, when the Moon's orbit takes it in front of Earth, it blocks the Sun from view, creating a solar eclipse. During a lunar eclipse, the opposite happens: Earth passes between the Sun and the Moon, casting a shadow on the Moon. A solar eclipse is visible only during the day, while a lunar eclipse is visible only at night. Lunar eclipses are more common and last longer than solar eclipses, and can be viewed from everywhere on the planet at night.

An eclipse may be partial, total, or annular (where one object covers all but the outer rim of another); and it may be barely noticeable or quite spectacular. The planes of Earth's orbit and the Moon's orbit

A total solar eclipse in La Paz, Baja California, Mexico, on July 11, 1991. *(Reproduced by permission of Photo Researchers, Inc.)*

Words to Know

Corona: The outermost atmospheric layer of the Sun.

Lunar eclipse: Occurs when Earth passes between the Sun and the Moon, casting a shadow on the Moon.

Penumbra: From Latin, meaning "almost shadow"; partial shadow surrounding the umbra during an eclipse.

Prominence: High-density cloud of gas projecting outward from the Sun's surface.

Solar eclipse: Occurs when the Moon passes between Earth and the Sun, casting a shadow on Earth.

Umbra: From Latin, meaning "shadow"; the completely dark portion of the shadow cast by Earth, the Moon, or other celestial body during an eclipse.

coincide only twice a year, signaling an eclipse season. Only during a small percentage of eclipse seasons do total eclipses occur.

Solar eclipses

During a solar eclipse, the Moon's shadow sweeps across Earth. The shadow has two parts: the dark, central part called the umbra, and the lighter region surrounding the umbra called the penumbra. Those people standing in a region covered by the umbra witness a total eclipse; those in the penumbra see only a partial eclipse.

The type of solar eclipse depends on the distance of the Moon from Earth. The Moon's orbit, like Earth's, is elliptical (oval-shaped). At some points along its orbit, the Moon is closer to Earth than at others. In order for a total eclipse to occur, with the umbra reaching Earth, the Moon must be at a close point on its orbit. If the Moon is too far away, it appears smaller than the Sun and one of two things may happen. First, only the penumbra may reach Earth, creating a partial eclipse. The other possibility is that the Moon will appear to be centered within the Sun. When this occurs, a ring of brilliant sunlight, like a ring of fire, appears around the rim of the Moon. This is known as an annular (ring) eclipse.

The first stage of a solar eclipse, when the Moon just begins to cover one edge of the Sun, is called first contact. As the Moon shifts across the Sun's face, the sky begins to darken. At the same time, bands of light and dark called shadow bands race across the ground. Just before second contact, when the Moon completely blocks out the Sun, a final flash of light can be seen at the edge of the Sun, an effect called the diamond ring.

Then, at totality, all sunlight is blocked, the sky turns dark, and the planets and brighter stars are visible. During this period, the Sun's corona, or outer atmosphere, is visible as a halo. The weak light given off by the corona (about half the light of a full moon) is normally not visible because it is overpowered by the light of the Sun's surface. Prominences, jets of gas that leap from the Sun's surface, are also visible during the total eclipse. After a few minutes, the Moon begins to pass to the other side of the Sun, signaling an end to the solar eclipse.

Lunar eclipses

A lunar eclipse can occur only when the Moon lies behind Earth, opposite the Sun, and is fully illuminated. As the Moon crosses into Earth's umbra, it does not become totally hidden. The reason is that gas molecules in Earth's atmosphere refract or bend the Sun's light around the surface of the planet, allowing some of it to reach the Moon. Because the wavelengths of red light are refracted less, the Moon will appear various shades of red during a lunar eclipse.

If the entire Moon falls within the umbra, the result is a total lunar eclipse. If only part of the Moon passes through the umbra, or if it only passes through the penumbra, a partial lunar eclipse occurs. A partial lunar eclipse may be difficult to detect since the Moon dims only slightly.

[See also **Calendar; Moon; Sun**]

Ecology

Ecology is the study of the relationships of organisms with their living and nonliving environment. No organism exists entirely independently of other living and nonliving things around it. A cactus in the middle of the desert, for example, draws nourishment from the air and from the ground. It depends on sunlight for energy needed to grow. The cactus may be home to birds, lizards, and microscopic animals. Even relationships that seem to be stark and simple as that of the cactus with its surroundings involve complex ties that form the subject matter of ecology.

Words to Know

Biosphere: The sum total of all life-forms on Earth and the interaction among those life-forms.

Community: A collection of populations that interacts with each other in the same geographic region.

Interdisciplinary: A field of investigation that draws upon knowledge from many disciplines.

Photosynthesis: The sequence of chemical reactions by which green plants convert carbon dioxide and water into starch and oxygen, using energy provided from sunlight.

Ecological relationships are always reciprocal (shared) relationships. In the example of the cactus, elements of the physical environment, such as air and water, have an impact on the cactus. But, at the same time, the cactus affects its physical surroundings. For example, it releases water vapor and oxygen into the air, changing the composition of the surrounding atmosphere.

Living relationships are also reciprocal relationships. The cactus may provide food, shelter, and shade for animals that live in or near it. But animals also contribute to the life of the cactus, by distributing its seeds, for example.

The subject matter of ecology

Although mostly a biological subject, ecology also draws upon other sciences, including chemistry, physics, geology, earth science, mathematics, computer science, and others. As the impact of humans on the environment increases, the subject matter of ecology expands. Ecologists may be asked to decide whether a desert should be left in its natural state or opened to certain forms of human development. As a result, ecologists increasingly find themselves confronted with social, economic, political, and other nonscientific issues. Because it draws upon knowledge and information from so many disciplines, ecology is a highly interdisciplinary field.

That ecologists focus on biological subjects is apparent from the fact that most ecologists spend much of their time engaged in studies of organisms. Examples of common themes of ecological research include: (1) how organisms adapt to their environment, (2) how the numbers and distribution patterns of organisms in an area are influenced by environmental factors, and (3) changes in the number of organisms in a area over time and how the environment influenced these changes.

Energy and productivity

One of the major areas of interest in ecology is the flow of energy through an ecosystem. (An ecosystem, or ecological system, is a collection of communities of organisms and the environment in which they live.) The source of almost all life on Earth is energy from the Sun, in the form of sunlight. That energy is captured by green plants in the process known as photosynthesis. When herbivorous (plant-eating) animals consume plants, they incorporate solar energy stored in those plants into their own bodies. Later, carnivorous (meat-eating) animals consume the herbivores, and solar energy is passed another step through the living world. Eventually, plants and animals die and are consumed by organisms known as decomposers (or detritivores; pronounced de-TRY-tuh-vorz). The complex of ecological relationships among all of the plants, animals, and decomposers is known as a food web.

A curved-bill thrasher perched near its nest in a cactus at the Arizona Sonora Desert Museum. Even relationships that seem to be stark, such as that of the cactus with its surroundings, involve complex ties that form the subject matter of ecology. *(Reproduced by permission of Field Mark Publications.)*

The ultimate goal of ecology

The ultimate goal of ecology is to understand the nature of environmental influences on individual organisms, their populations and communities, on landscapes and, ultimately, the biosphere (all life on Earth). If ecologists can achieve an understanding of these relationships, they will be able to contribute to the development of systems by which humans will be able to wisely use ecological resources, such as forests, agricultural soils, and hunted animals such as deer and fish. This goal is a very important one because humans are, after all, completely reliant on ecological goods and services as their only source of life support.

[*See also* **Biome; Biosphere; Ecosystem; Environmental ethics**]

Ecosystem

An ecosystem (or ecological system) is a collection of communities of organisms and the environment in which they live. Ecosystems can vary greatly in size. Some examples of small ecosystems are tidal pools, a home garden, or the stomach of an individual cow. Larger ecosystems might encompass lakes, agricultural fields, or stands of forests. Landscape-scale ecosystems encompass larger regions, and may include different terrestrial (land) and aquatic (water) communities. Ultimately, all of Earth's life and its physical environment could be considered to represent an entire ecosystem, known as the biosphere.

Ecologists often invent boundaries for ecosystems, depending on the particular needs of their work. (Ecologists are scientists who study the relationships of organisms with their living and nonliving environments.) For example, depending on the specific interests of an ecologist, an ecosystem might be defined as the shoreline vegetation around a lake, or the entire lake itself, or the lake plus all the land around it. Because all of these units consist of organisms and their environment, they can properly be considered to be ecosystems.

The raw materials of an ecosystem

All ecosystems have a few basic characteristics in common. They use energy (usually provided by sunlight) to build complex chemical compounds out of simple materials. At the level of plants, for example, carbon dioxide and water vapor are combined with the energy of sunlight to produce complex carbohydrates, such as starches (this process is known as photosynthesis). As plants (producers) are consumed by other organisms, more complex substances are manufactured in their bodies, and energy is passed upward through the food web.

The flow of energy in an ecosystem occurs in only one direction: it is always consumed by higher levels of organisms in a food web. As a result, each level of a food web contains less energy than the levels below it. By contrast, nutrients can flow in any direction in an ecosystem. When plants and animals die, the compounds of which they are formed are decomposed by microorganisms (decomposers), returned to the environment, and are recycled for use again by other organisms.

One of the greatest challenges facing humans and their civilization is to develop an understanding of the fundamentals of ecosystem organization, how they function and how they are structured. This knowledge

A freshwater ecosystem.
(Reproduced by permission of The Gale Group.)

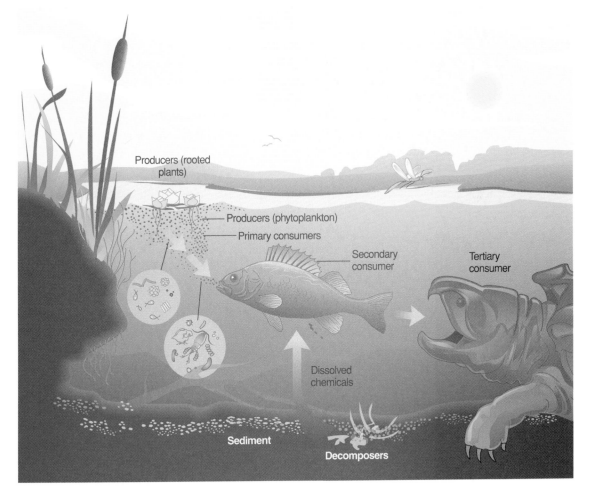

is absolutely necessary if humans are to design systems that allow for the continued use of the products and services of ecosystems. Humans are sustained by ecosystems, and no alternative to this relationship exists.

[*See also* **Biosphere; Gaia hypothesis**]

Elasticity

Just about every solid material possesses some degree of elasticity, and so do most liquids. Some common highly elastic products are rubber bands, kitchen spatulas, and bicycle tires. Even buildings and bridges have some degree of elasticity (or give) so they can adjust to small shifts in Earth's surface.

Chemical principles

Elasticity is a chemical property that allows a solid body to return to its original shape after an outside force is removed. The key to determining whether a substance is elastic is to apply a force to it. With sufficient force, the substance should change its size, shape, or volume. If, when the force is removed, the sample returns to its original state, then it is elastic. If the substance returns only partially (or not at all) to its original state, it is called inelastic.

If too much force is applied, the material is in danger of reaching its elastic limit. The elastic limit is the point at which the material is bent beyond its ability to return to its original shape. Once the elastic limit is passed, the material will experience permanent reshaping, called plastic deformation, and will no longer act as an elastic substance.

This stretching/recoiling activity is easily seen by hanging a weight from a spring: if the weight is within the spring's elastic capacity, the spring will bounce back (in an elastic manner). However, if the weight is too heavy for the spring, the weight will pull the spring straight, making it inelastic. (Think of a Slinky™, the coiled wire toy that travels down stairs and then regains its original shape. If too much force is applied to it, the Slinky™ becomes bent out of shape or inelastic.)

Elasticity works because of two basic forces that operate at the molecular level: attracting force and repelling force. When at rest, these forces within the molecules balance each other. By adding a compressing force (say, by squeezing a spring), the repelling force increases in an attempt to once again balance the system. Likewise, by adding a stretching force

Words to Know

Strain: The amount by which a material stretches divided by its original length.

Stress: The force applied to an object divided by the area on which the force operates.

(as in a weight pulling a spring), the attracting force increases, causing the elastic material to bounce back.

Early experiments

The first scientist to conduct in-depth research into the behavior of elastic materials was the famous English physicist Robert Hooke (1635–1703). Through experiments Hooke discovered that the relationship between tension (the force applied) and extension (the amount of bending that is produced) is directly proportional. For example, a weight will stretch a spring, and a weight twice as heavy will stretch it twice as much. Hooke's research has since been combined into a series of mathematical principles known as Hooke's law.

More than 100 years after Hooke's studies, another English scientist, Thomas Young, discovered that different elastic materials bend to different degrees when a force is applied. For example, brass bends more than lead, but less than rubber. The amount of elasticity of a particular material, Young found, can be expressed as a constant called Young's modulus. Knowledge of Young's modulus is essential to modern architects, who must be able to predict how construction materials will act when they are under stress.

Electrical conductivity

Electrical conductivity is the ability of a material to carry the flow of an electric current (a flow of electrons). Imagine that you attach the two ends of a battery to a bar of iron and a galvanometer. (A galvanometer is an instrument for measuring the flow of electric current.) When this con-

▼ Electrical Resistance

Another way of describing the conductivity of a material is through resistance. Resistance can be defined as the extent to which a material prevents the flow of electricity. Silver, aluminum, iron and other metals have a low resistance (and a high conductivity). Wood, paper, and most plastics have a high resistance (and a low conductivity).

The unit of measurement for electrical resistance is called the ohm (abbreviation: Ω). The ohm was named for German physicist Georg Simon Ohm (1789–1854), who first expressed the mathematical laws of electrical conductance and resistance in detail. Interestingly enough, the unit of electrical conductance is called the mho (ohm written backwards). This choice of units clearly illustrates the reciprocal (opposite) relationship between electrical resistance and conductivity.

nection is made, the galvanometer shows that electric current is flowing through the iron bar. The iron bar can be said to be a conductor of electric current.

Replacing the iron bar in this system with other materials produces different galvanometer readings. Other metals also conduct an electric current, but to different extents. If a bar of silver or aluminum is used, the galvanometer shows a greater flow of electrical current than with the iron bar. Silver and aluminum are better conductors of electricity than is iron. If a lead bar is inserted, the galvanometer shows a lower reading than with iron. Lead is a poorer conductor of electricity than are silver, aluminum, or iron.

Many materials can be substituted for the original iron bar that will produce a zero reading on the galvanometer. These materials do not permit the flow of electric current at all. They are said to be nonconductors, or insulators. Wood, paper, and most plastics are common examples of insulators.

How conductance takes place

Electrical conductivity occurs because of the ease with which electrons can be removed from atoms. All substances consist of atoms. In turn, all atoms consist of two main parts: a positively charged nucleus and one or more negatively charged electrons. An atom of iron, for example, consists of a nucleus with 26 positive charges and 26 negatively charged electrons.

The electrons in an atom are not all held with equal strength. Electrons close to the nucleus are strongly attracted by the positive charge of the nucleus and are removed from the atom only with great difficulty. Electrons farthest from the nucleus are held only loosely and are removed quite easily.

A block of iron can be thought of as a huge collection of iron atoms. Most of the electrons in these atoms are held tightly by the iron nuclei. But a few electrons are held loosely—so loosely that they act as if they don't even belong to atoms at all. Scientists sometimes refer to this condition as a cloud of electrons.

Normally these "free" electrons have no place to go. They just spin around randomly among the iron atoms. That situation changes, however, when a battery (or other source of electric current) is attached to the iron block. Electrons flow out of one end of the battery and into the other. At the electron-rich end of the battery, electrons flow into the piece of iron, pushing iron electrons ahead of them. Since all electrons have the same negative charge, they repel each other. Iron electrons are pushed away from the electron-rich end of the battery towards the electron-poor end. In other words, an electric current flows through the iron.

Insulators have a very different structure. They too consist of atoms (nuclei and electrons), but very few free electrons can be found in insulators. Those electrons tend to be bound tightly to nuclei in chemical bonds. Attaching a battery to an insulator has no effect since there are no free electrons to be pushed through the material.

Solution conductivity

Electrons are not the only particles capable of carrying an electric current. Ions can do it, too. An ion is an atom or group of atoms with an electric charge. Suppose you dissolve a crystal of table salt (sodium chloride) in water. Salt crystals consist of positive sodium ions and negative chloride ions. In the solid state, these ions are not free to move around. Once they are dissolved in water, however, they become completely mobile. They are free to "swim" about in the water and to respond to an electric current from a battery. That current supplies electrons that cause positive sodium ions to flow in one direction and negative chloride ions to flow in the opposite direction.

A good example of this effect can be seen in the conductivity of water. Pure water consists only of water molecules. The electrons in water molecules are held tightly by hydrogen and oxygen atoms and are not free to move. Attaching a battery to a container of water produces no electric current because pure water is an insulator. But a few grains of table salt added to the water changes things completely. Sodium ions and chloride ions are released from the salt, and the salt water solution becomes conductive.

Semiconductivity and superconductivity

Some materials cannot be classified as either conductors or insulators. Semiconductors, for example, are materials that conduct an electric current but do so very poorly. Semiconductors were not well understood until the mid-twentieth century, when a series of remarkable discoveries revolutionized the field of electrical conductivity. These discoveries have made possible a virtually limitless variety of electronic devices, ranging from miniature radios and handheld calculators to massive solar power arrays and orbiting telescopes.

Superconductivity is a property that appears only at very low temperatures, usually close to absolute zero (−273°C). At such temperatures, certain materials lose all resistance to electric current; they become perfect conductors. Once an electric current is initiated in such materials, it continues to flow without diminishing and can go on essentially forever.

The discovery of superconductivity holds enormous potential for the development of electric appliances. In such appliances, a large fraction of the electrical energy supplied to the device is lost in overcoming electrical resistance within the device. That lost energy shows up as waste heat. If the same appliance were made of a superconducting material, no energy would be lost because there would be no resistance to overcome. The appliance would become, at least in principle, 100 percent efficient.

[See also **Superconductor**]

Electric arc

An electric arc is a device in which an electric current (a flow of electrons) is caused to flow between two points separated by a gas. The two points are called electrodes. The one from which the current originates is the cathode. The electrode toward which electrons flow is the anode. The term electric arc refers both to the device itself as well as to the electric discharge that takes place within the device. Arcs can make use of high, atmospheric, or low pressures and can contain a variety of gases. They have wide uses as luminous lamps; as furnaces; for heating, cutting, and welding; and as tools for certain kinds of chemical analysis.

Electrical conductivity in gases

Gases are normally poor conductors of electricity. The atoms or molecules of which they consist usually contain no free electrons needed for a current to flow. That condition can change, however. If sufficient energy is supplied to the gas, its atoms or molecules will break apart (ionize) into charged particles. If a spark is passed through a container of oxygen gas, for example, oxygen molecules ionize to form some positively charged oxygen ions and some negatively charged oxygen ions. These charged particles then make it possible for the gas to become conductive.

Arc construction

In an electric arc, the energy needed to produce ionization comes from an external source, such as an electric generator. An intense stream of electrons flows into the cathode and then across the gas-filled gap to the anode. As these electrons pass through the gas, they cause ionization. Ions formed in the process make the flow of current between electrodes even easier. For every gas, some minimum amount of energy is needed

Illustration of an electric arc between two metals. *(Reproduced by permission of Photo Researchers, Inc.)*

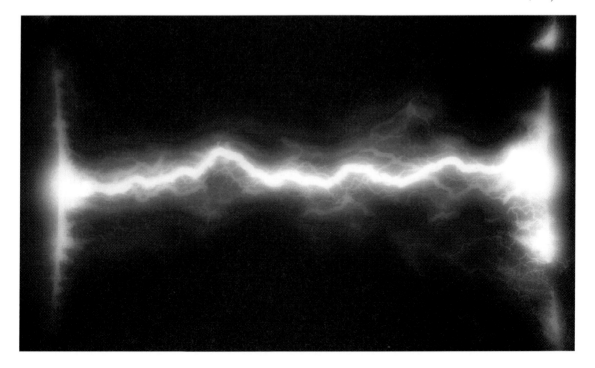

to produce ionization at a given temperature and pressure. That energy is known as the gas's breakdown potential.

One example of an electric arc is a lightning bolt. In nature, two clouds can act as electrodes, or electric current may flow between a cloud and Earth's surface. In either case, current flows through the air, ionizing molecules of oxygen, nitrogen, and other gases in the atmosphere.

The light and sound associated with lightning are evidence of an important change that occurs in the gas between electrodes. The flow of electric current heats the gas to high temperatures. The light associated with lightning is evidence of that change. The clap of thunder is another sign of the change—the heated air around the lightning bolt expands rapidly, producing a sound wave.

The simplest electric arc consists of two electrodes made of a conducting material and situated a short distance from each other. Air is the gas used in this arc. This kind of electric arc was first studied by English physicist and chemist Humphry Davy (1778–1829) in 1808.

Various types of electric arcs differ from each other in two respects: the pressure at which they operate and the materials of which they are made. Electric arcs can be enclosed in glass or plastic containers from which air has been pumped out (vacuum arcs) or to which air or some other gas has been added (high pressure arcs).

The light produced by an arc depends both on the material from which the electrodes are made and on the gas that separates them. Some electrodes have no function other than to conduct an electric current into and out of the arc. Other electrodes are chosen because they tend to vaporize when the arc is used, changing the discharge that is produced. Various gases are chosen for use in electric arcs because they too affect the discharges produced. For instance, each chemical element produces its own characteristic color when ionized.

Uses of electric arcs

Many types of arcs exist, each with its own applications. For example, arc welders are used for welding (where a metal is fused and added in a joint). In some cases, the arc's only function is to supply heat. In other cases, the metal from one electrode may actually be used in forming the weld. Plasma torches are used for cutting, spraying, and gas heating. Plasma is a term used for hot, ionized gases. Cutting a metal with a plasma torch may be done by means of an arc formed between the metal itself and an electrode from the torch.

Electric arcs are often used as lamps because of the amount of light they produce. That light comes from hot, glowing electrodes (carbon arcs) and, sometimes, from heated gases (flame arcs). The carbon arc, in which two carbon rods serve as electrodes, was the first practical commercial lighting device. It remains one of the brightest sources of light and is still used in theater motion-picture projectors, large searchlights, and lighthouses. Flame arcs are used in color photography and in photochemical processes because they closely approximate natural sunshine. The carbon is saturated with chemicals that boil off easily. These chemicals become luminous when they evaporate and are heated by the arc.

The color of flame arcs depends on the material of which the electrodes are made. For example, calcium arcs give off a red glow, while barium arcs give off a green glow. In some flame arcs, the radiation produced is outside the visible range. Mercury arcs at high pressure produce ultraviolet radiation. They also can produce visible light in a low pressure tube if the internal walls of the tube are coated with a fluorescent material known as a phosphor. The phosphor emits visible light when struck by ultraviolet radiation from the mercury.

Arcs can also be used in radio valves, such as those used in the early days of radio, and as a source of ions in nuclear reactors and thermonuclear devices (devices for controlling the release of nuclear power).

[*See also* **Electricity; Electronics**]

Electric current

An electric current is usually thought of as a flow of electrons. When two ends of a battery are connected to each other by means of a metal wire, electrons flow out of one end (electrode or pole) of the battery, through the wire, and into the opposite end of the battery.

An electric current can also be thought of as a flow of positive "holes." A "hole" in this sense is a region of space where an electron might normally be found but does not exist. The absence of the electron's negative charge can be thought of as creating a positively charged hole.

In some cases, an electric current can also consist of a flow of positively charge particles known as cations. A cation is simply an atom or group of atoms carrying a positive charge.

Current measurement

The ampere (amp) is used to measure the amount of current flow. The unit was named for French mathematician and physicist André Marie Ampère (1775–1836), who founded the modern study of electric currents.

The ampere is defined in terms of the number of electrons that pass any given point in some unit of time. Since electric charge is measured in coulombs, an exact definition for the ampere is the number of coulombs that pass a given point each second.

Characteristics of an electric current

Potential difference.   In order for an electric current to flow, a number of conditions must be met. First, a potential difference must exist between two points. The term potential difference (or voltage) means that the force created by a group of electrons in one place is greater than the force of electrons in some other place. The greater force pushes electrons away from the first place and toward the second place.

Potential differences usually do not occur in nature. In most cases, the distribution of electrons in the world around us is fairly even. Scientists have invented certain kinds of devices, however, in which electrons can be accumulated, producing a potential difference. A battery, for example, is nothing other than a device for producing large masses of electrons at one electrode (a point from which electric current is sent or received) and a deficiency of electrons at the other electrode. This difference accounts for the battery's ability to generate a potential difference, or voltage.

Electrical resistance.   A second condition needed in order for a current to flow is a path along which electrons can travel. Some materials are able to provide such a path, and others are not. Materials that permit a flow of electric current are said to be conductors. Those that block the flow of electric current are called nonconductors or insulators. The metal wire connecting the two battery poles in the example cited earlier provides a path for the movement of electrons from one pole of the battery to the other.

The conductivity of materials is an intrinsic (or natural) property based on their resistance to the movement of electrons. The electrons in some materials are tied up in chemical bonds and are not available to conduct an electric current. In other materials, large numbers of electrons are free to move, and they transmit a flow of electrons easily.

Electrical resistance (or resistivity) is measured in a unit known as the ohm (Ω). The unit was named in honor of German physicist Georg Simon Ohm (1789–1854), the first person to express the laws of electrical conductivity. The opposite of resistance is conductance, a property that is measured in a unit called the mho (ohm spelled backwards).

The resistance of a piece of wire used in an electric circuit depends on three factors: the length of the wire, its cross-sectional area, and the resistivity of the material of which the wire is made. To understand the effects of electrical resistance, think of water flowing through a hose.

The amount of water that flows through the hose is similar to the current in the wire. Just as more water can pass through a fat fire hose than a skinny garden hose, a fat metal wire can carry more current than a skinny metal wire. For the wire, the larger the cross-sectional area, the lower its resistance; the smaller the cross-sectional area, the greater its resistance.

A similar comparison can be made with regard to length. It is harder for water to flow through a long hose simply because it has to travel farther. Similarly, it is harder for current to travel through a long wire than through a short wire.

Resistivity is a property of the material of which the wire itself is made and differs from material to material. Imagine filling a fire hose with molasses rather than water. The molasses will flow more slowly simply because of its viscosity (stickiness or resistance to flow). Similarly, electric current flows through some metals (such as lead) with more difficulty than it does through other metals (such as silver).

Electric circuits

In most cases, the path followed by an electric current is known as an electric circuit. At a minimum, a circuit consists of (1) a source of electrons (such as a battery) that will provide a potential difference and (2) a pathway on which the electrons can travel (such as a metal wire). Recall that potential difference (or voltage) refers to a greater force of electrons in one place than in another; that greater force propels electrons toward the place with the lower force.

For any practical (or useful) application, a current also requires (3) an appliance whose operation depends on a flow of electric current. Such appliances include electric clocks, toasters, radios, television sets, and various types of electric motors. In many cases, electric circuits also contain (4) some kind of meter that shows the amount of electric current or potential difference in a circuit. Finally, a circuit is likely to include (5) various devices to control the flow of electric current, such as rectifiers, transformers, condensers, and circuit breakers.

Appliances may be placed into an electric circuit in one of two ways. In a series circuit, current flows through the appliances one after the other. In a parallel circuit, an incoming current is divided up and sent through each separate circuit independently.

An important advantage of parallel circuits is their resistance to damage. Suppose that any one of the appliances in a series circuit is damaged so that current cannot flow through it. This breakdown prevents current from flowing in any of the appliances. Such a problem does not arise with a parallel circuit. If any one of the appliances in a parallel circuit fails, current still continues to flow through the other appliances in the circuit.

The principle mathematical relationship governing the flow of electric current in a circuit was discovered by Ohm in 1827. Ohm's law states that the amount of current (i) in a circuit is directly related to the potential difference (V) and inversely related to the resistance (r) in the circuit. In other words, $i = V/r$. What Ohm's law says is that an increase in po-

This electric circuit will be used as a control panel in an industrial system. *(Reproduced by permission of The Stock Market.)*

tential difference or a decrease in resistance produces an increase in current flow. Conversely, a decrease in potential difference or an increase in resistance produces a decrease in current flow. The more complicated an electric circuit becomes, the more difficult it becomes to apply Ohm's law.

Current flow and electron flow

The field of electrical engineering is burdened with a strange problem that developed more than 200 years ago. When scientists first studied the flow of electric current from one place to another, they believed that the flow was produced by the motion of tiny particles. Since the electron had not yet been discovered, they assumed that those particles carried a positive charge.

Today we know otherwise. Electric current is a flow of negatively charged particles: electrons. But the custom of showing electric current as positive has been around for a long time, and it is still widely used. For that reason, it is not uncommon to see electric current represented as a flow of positive charges, even though we have known better for a long time.

Direct and alternating current

The type of electric current described thus far is direct current (DC current). Direct current always involves the movement of electrons from a region of high negative charge to one of lower negative charge. The electric current produced by batteries is direct current.

Interestingly enough, the vast majority of electric current used for practical purposes is alternating current (AC current). Alternating current is current that changes the direction in which it flows very quickly. In North America, for example, commercial electrical power lines operate at a frequency of 60 hertz. (Hertz is the unit of frequency.) In a 60 hertz line, the current changes its direction 60 times every second.

Other types of alternating current also are used widely. Outside of North America, a 50 hertz power line is more common. And in airplanes, alternating current is usually rated at 400 hertz.

[*See also* **Electricity; Electric motor**]

Electricity

Electricity is a form of energy caused by the presence of electrical charges in matter. All matter consists of atoms, and atoms themselves contain charged particles. Each proton in an atomic nucleus carries one unit of positive electric charge, and each electron circling a nucleus carries one unit of negative electric charge. Electrical phenomena occur when electrons escape from atoms. The loss of one or more electrons (negative charges) from an atom leaves behind a positively charged fragment known as a positive ion. An electric current is produced when a mass of electrons released from atoms begins to flow.

Static and current electricity

Electrical phenomena can be classified in one of two general categories: static electricity or current electricity. The term static electricity refers to the behavior of electrical charges at rest. Suppose you hang two ping-pong balls from silk threads so that they are about 2 inches (5 centimeters) apart. Then imagine that each ball is rubbed with a piece of wool. The two balls become electrically charged with the same sign. Because like charges repel each other, the two balls will swing away from each other because of the static charge on each one.

Current electricity refers to the behavior of electrical charges in motion. In order for charged particles to flow, some pathway must be pro-

A Van de Graaff generator is a device that is capable of building up a very high potential for static electricity. In this photo, the charge that has accumulated in the generator's dome is leaking into the hair of a wig that has been placed on top of the generator. Because the hairs are similarly charged and like charges repel each other, the hairs repel each other. *(Reproduced by permission of Photo Researchers, Inc.)*

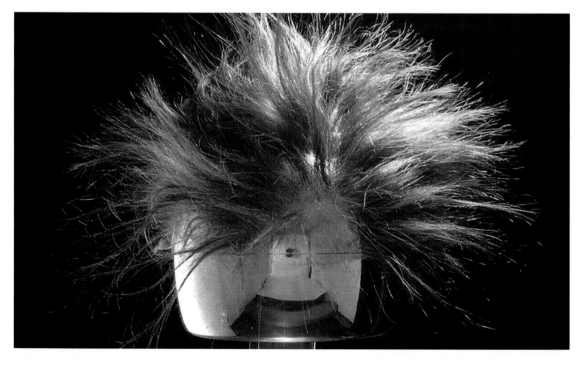

vided for them. That pathway is called an electric circuit. An electric circuit typically consists of a source of electricity, such as a battery; an appliance that operates on electric energy, such as a toaster; a meter that measures the flow of electrons, such as a galvanometer; and metal wires connecting those parts of the circuit.

Electric charge

The two kinds of electric charges—positive and negative—have the same magnitude (size, force, or intensity) but opposite effects. The magnitude of an electric charge has been measured very accurately and been found to be 1.602189×10^{-19} coulomb. The unit used in measuring electric charge (coulomb; C) was named after French physicist Charles Augustin de Coulomb (1736–1806), an early authority on electrical theory. The coulomb is a fundamental property of matter, like the mass of an electron, the gravitational constant, and the speed of light.

Since a single positive charge and a single negative charge have the same magnitude, their combination produces a net charge of zero. That is, $+1.602189 \times 10^{-19}$ C $+ -1.602189 \times 10^{-19}$ C $= 0$. All atoms normally have equal numbers of protons and electrons and are, therefore, electrically neutral. This fact explains the absence of electrical phenomena in everyday life. A person walking across ordinary grass normally does not get a shock because grass, dirt, and air are all made of electrically neutral atoms.

Only when electrons or protons begin to accumulate do electrical events occur. One such effect can be observed when a person shuffles across a carpet. Friction transfers charges between shoe soles and carpet, resulting in the familiar electrical shock when the excess charge sparks to a nearby person. Lightning is another phenomenon caused by the accumulation of electric charges. At some point, those charges become so large that they jump from one cloud to another cloud—or between ground and cloud—producing a lightning bolt.

Electric fields

Any charged particle alters the space around it. For comparison, think of any object in space, such as a planet. The region around that object (in this case, the space around the planet) is affected by the object's (the planet's) presence. We call that effect gravity. A second object placed in the gravitational field of the first object is attracted to the first object. A space probe sent in the direction of another planet, for example, is pulled toward that planet's surface by gravitational attraction.

Electric charges have similar effects. Imagine a ping-pong ball carrying a negative charge is suspended in the air by means of a silk thread. Then, a second ping-pong ball is placed in the vicinity of (or near to) the first ball. The second ping-pong ball will be attracted to or repelled by the first ping-pong ball. The second ball experiences a force of attraction or repulsion caused by the nature of the electric charge on the first ball. The region in space over which that force exists is called an electric field.

Coulomb's law

The law describing the force between charged particles was discovered by Coulomb in 1777. Electrical force, Coulomb found, depends on two factors: the electric charge on any two objects and the distance between them. That force can be expressed as an inverse square law. That is, the force between two charged particles decreases as the distance between them increases. When the distance is doubled (increased by 2), the force is reduced by one-fourth ($\frac{1}{2}^2$). When the distance is tripled, the force is reduced by one-ninth ($\frac{1}{3}^3$). And when the distance is made ten times as great, the forced is reduced by $\frac{1}{100}$ ($\frac{1}{10}^2$).

Electrical properties

Potential difference.   Any collection of electric charges (such as a large mass of electrons) has certain characteristic properties, including potential difference and current flow. Potential difference, also called voltage, is the amount of electric energy stored in a mass of electric charges compared to the energy stored in some other mass of charges.

Imagine a small box into which electrons can be pumped. Pushing the first few electrons into the box is not difficult. But the more electrons in the box, the more difficult it is to add additional electrons. Electrons are all negatively charged, so they repel each other. Adding electron number 1,001 to the box, for example, is difficult because it must overcome the repulsion of 1,000 electrons already in the box. Adding electron number 10,001 is even more difficult.

The more electrons that have been accumulated, therefore, the greater their pressure to escape. The giant spark machines that are sometimes displayed at science fairs illustrate this point. Electrons are added to one of two large metal balls that make up the machine. Normally the air between the two balls is a nonconductor of electricity: it does not permit the flow of electrons from one ball to the other. At some point, however, the number of electrons on the first ball becomes too large to maintain this nonconductive state—the potential difference between it and the second ball is just too great. Many electrons jump all at once from the first ball to the second ball, producing a giant electric spark.

Potential difference is responsible for the operation of all electric appliances. Electric power companies build power plants where huge amounts of electric charge are accumulated; in other words, these plants are capable of providing high voltage electric currents. When a consumer turns on a switch, a pathway for that current is provided. Electric charges

Electricity arcing over the surface of ceramic insulators. *(Reproduced by permission of The Stock Market.)*

rush out of the power plant, through transmission wires, and into the consumer's home. There they flow through and turn on a microwave, a CD player, a television set, a VCR, or some other electric device.

Electric current. The rate at which electric charges flow through a circuit is called current. The formal definition of current (designated by the symbol i) is the number of electric charges (C) that pass a given point in a circuit (a path of current that includes a power source) per second (t). Mathematically, $i = C/t$.

The unit of current flow is the ampere (amp, or A), named for French physicist André Marie Ampère (1775–1836). One ampere is defined as the flow of one coulomb (a measurement of electrical charge) of electrons per second.

Electrical resistance. The flow of electrons in a circuit depends on two factors. One factor is the potential difference or voltage in the circuit. The other factor is resistance, a force similar to mechanical friction that reduces the flow of electrons through a material. Nearly all materials have at least some resistance to the flow of electric current. Those with a smaller resistance are said to be conductors of electricity. Those with a greater resistance are called nonconductors, or insulators. The unit of electrical resistance is the ohm (Ω), named for German physicist Georg Simon Ohm (1789–1854).

The amount of current that flows through an electric circuit can be expressed mathematically by a law discovered by Ohm in 1827. Ohm's law says that the amount of current in a circuit is equal to the potential difference in the circuit divided by the electrical resistance, or $i = V/r$.

Electric power

The most useful way of expressing the amount of work available from an electric current is electric power. Electric power is defined as the product of the voltage and current in a circuit, or: $P = V \cdot i$. Thus, a circuit with a high potential difference (voltage) and a large current is a source of a large electric power.

Most people are familiar with the unit for electric power, the watt (W). The watt was named for English inventor James Watt (1736–1819). One watt is defined as the product of one volt times one ampere, or $1 \text{ W} = 1 \text{ V} \times 1 \text{ A}$.

Most electric appliances are rated according to the electric power needed to operate them. Ordinary lightbulbs, for example, are likely to be 25 W, 60 W, or 100 W bulbs. At the end of each month, local electric companies send consumers a bill for the amount of electric power used during that time. The bill is based on the number of kilowatts (thousands of watts) and the price per kilowatt in the consumers' area.

Electric motor

An electric motor is a device used to convert electrical energy to mechanical energy. Electric motors are extremely important in modern-day life. They are used in vacuum cleaners, dishwashers, computer printers, fax machines, video cassette recorders, machine tools, printing presses, automobiles, subway systems, sewage treatment plants, and water pumping stations, to mention only a few applications.

Principle of operation

The basic principle on which motors operate is Ampere's law. This law states that a wire carrying an electric current produces a magnetic field around itself. Imagine that current is flowing through

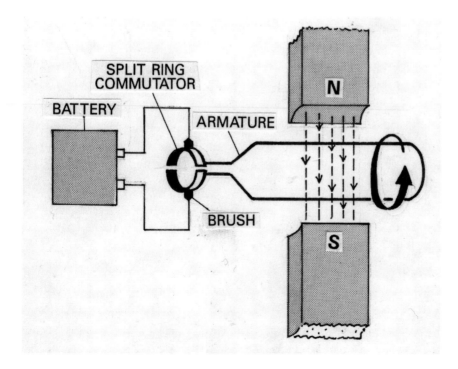

A figure of an electric motor. *(Reproduced by permission of The Gale Group.)*

the wire loop shown in the figure below. The presence of that current creates a magnetic field around the wire. Since the loop itself has become a magnet, one side of it will be attracted to the north (N) pole of the surrounding magnet and the other side will be attracted to the south (S) pole of the magnet. The loop will begin to rotate, as shown by the arrow marked F.

AC motors. What happens next depends on the kind of electric current used to run the motor, direct (DC) or alternating (AC) current. With AC current, the direction in which the current flows changes back and forth rapidly and at a regular rate. In the United States, the rate of change is 60 times per second, or 60 hertz (the unit of frequency).

In an AC motor, then, the current flows first in one direction through the wire loop and then reverses itself about 1/60 second later. This change of direction means that the magnetic field produced around the loop also changes once every 1/60 second. At one instant, one part of the loop is attracted by the north pole of the magnet, and at the next instant, it is attracted by the south pole of the magnet.

But this shifting of the magnetic field is necessary to keep the motor operating. When the current is flowing in one direction, the right hand side of the coil might become the south pole of the loop magnet. It would be repelled by the south pole of the outside magnet and attracted by the north pole of the outside magnet. The wire loop would be twisted around until the right side of the loop had completed half a revolution and was next to the north pole of the outside magnet.

If nothing further happened, the loop would come to a stop, since two opposite magnetic poles—one from the outside magnet and one from the wire loop—would be adjacent to (located next to) each other. And unlike magnetic poles attract each other. But something further does happen. The current changes direction, and so does the magnetic field around the wire loop. The side of the loop that was previously attracted to the north pole is now attracted to the south pole, and vice versa. Therefore, the loop receives another "kick," twisting it around on its axis in response to the new forces of magnetic attraction and repulsion.

Thus, as long as the current continues to change direction, the wire loop is forced to spin around on its axis. This spinning motion can be used to operate any one of the electrical appliances mentioned above.

DC motors. When electric motors were first invented, AC current had not yet been discovered. So the earliest motors all operated on DC current, such as the current provided by a battery.

Capacitor

A capacitor is a device for storing electrical energy. Capacitors are used in a wide variety of applications today. Engineers use large banks of capacitors, for example, to test the performance of an electrical circuit when struck by a bolt of lighting. The energy released by these large capacitors is similar to the lightning bolt. On another scale, a camera flash works by storing energy in a capacitor and then releasing it to cause a quick bright flash of light. On the smallest scale, capacitors are used in computer systems. A charged capacitor represents the number 1 and an uncharged capacitor a 0 in the binary number system used by computers.

How a capacitor stores energy A capacitor consists of two electrical conductors that are not in contact. The conductors are usually separated by a layer of insulating material known as a dielectric. Since air is a dielectric, an additional insulating material may not have to be added to the capacitor.

Think of a capacitor as consisting of two copper plates separated by 1 centimeter of air. Then imagine that electrical charge (that is, electrons) are pumped into one of the plates. That plate becomes negatively charged because of the excess number of electrons it contains. The negative charge on the first copper plate then induces (creates) a positive charge on the second plate.

As electrons are added to the first plate, one might expect a current to flow from that plate to the second plate. But the presence of the dielectric prevents any flow of electrical current. Instead, as more electrons are added to the first plate, it accumulates more and more energy. Adding electrons increases energy because each electron added to the plate has to overcome repulsion from other electrons already there. The tenth electron added has to bring with it more energy to add to the plate than did the fifth electron. And the one-hundredth electron will have to bring with it even more energy. As a result, as long as current flows into the first plate, it stores up more and more electrical energy.

Capacitors release the energy stored within them when the two plates are connected with each other. For example, just closing an electric switch between the two plates releases the energy stored in the first plate. That energy rushes through the circuit, providing a burst of energy.

Words to Know

Alternating current (AC): Electric current in which the direction of flow changes back and forth rapidly and at a regular rate.

Ampere's law: A law that states that a wire carrying an electric current produces a magnetic field around itself.

Direct current (DC): Electric current in which the direction of flow is always the same.

Frequency: The number of waves that pass a given point in a given period of time.

Hertz (Hz): The unit of frequency; a measure of the number of waves that pass a given point per second of time.

Split-ring commutator: A device that changes the direction of current flow in a DC motor.

The primary difference between a DC motor and an AC motor is finding a way to change the direction of current flow. In direct current, electric current always moves in the same direction. That means that the wire loop in the motor will stop turning after the first half revolution. Because the current is always flowing in the same direction, the resulting magnetic field always points in the same direction.

To solve this problem, the wire coming from the DC power source is attached to a metal ring cut in half, as shown in the figure. The ring is called a split-ring commutator. At the first moment the motor is turned on, current flows out of the battery, through the wire, and into one side of the commutator. The current then flows into the wire loop, producing a magnetic field.

Once the loop begins to rotate, however, it carries the commutator with it. After a half turn, the ring reaches the empty space in the two halves and then moves on to the second half of the commutator. At that point, then, current begins to flow into the opposite side of the loop, producing the same effect achieved with AC current. Current flows backward through the loop, the magnetic field is reversed, and the loop continues to rotate.

[*See also* **Electric current**]

Electrocardiogram

An electrocardiogram (pronounced ee-lek-troe-KAR-dee-oh-gram) is a recording of the electrical activity within the heart that is obtained by placing various electrodes on the skin surface. From this painless, quick, and inexpensive test, doctors are able to evaluate a person's heart rate and rhythm and to detect if something is wrong.

Normal and abnormal wave patterns

An electrocardiogram, better known as an EKG or ECG, is a common test doctors use to obtain information about the overall health of a patient's heart. Using a machine called an electrocardiograph, the physician is able to see a real-time image of the electrical activity going on in the heart. Usually the doctor examines a printed pattern of heart activity that is recorded on a moving strip of paper, but he or she may also view the pattern on a television-like screen. By examining this pattern of waves, the physician views an actual picture of the heart's rhythm and can then detect many heart problems. Since a normal, healthy heart makes a specific pattern of waves, a damaged or diseased heart changes that pattern in recognizable ways. Simply by examining the EKG, a physician can detect and analyze something like an abnormal or irregular heart rhythm known as an arrhythmia (pronounced uh-RITH-mee-uh). The physician can also identify areas of the heart muscle that have been damaged by coronary heart disease, high blood pressure, rheumatic fever, or birth defects. A previous heart attack will also show up on the pattern, and follow-up EKGs will show if the heart is recovering from it. An EKG also may be used to determine the effect of certain drugs on the heart, and is sometimes used to test how an implanted pacemaker is working.

First EKG

Physicians have not always been able to learn so much about the heart by viewing a simple printout of its electrical activity. The technique known as electrocardiography (pronounced ee-lek-troe-kar-dee-AH-gruh-fee) was first reported in 1901. In that year, Dutch physiologist William Einthoven (1860–1927) published a report documenting his invention of what was called the "string galvanometer." Einthoven was able to design such a device more than a hundred years ago because scientists knew by then that there was some sort of electrical activity going on in the heart. Earlier research done by Italian anatomist Luigi Galvani (1737–1798) and

▼ Words to Know

Arrhythmia: An irregular beating of the heart.

Depolarization: The tendency of a cell membrane when stimulated to allow ions to enter or leave the cell.

Ion: An atom or groups of atoms that carries an electrical charge—either positive or negative—as a result of losing or gaining one or more electrons.

Italian physicist Alessandro Volta (1745–1827) had proven that electricity does exist in living tissue. Although many had tried before him, Einthoven was the first to devise the best method for recording the electrical activity of the heart.

Electricity in living tissue

Although Galvani was able to demonstrate with his 1794 experiments the existence of electricity in living tissue, it was not until 1834 that anyone was able to record and measure that force. Even then, however, another three generations would pass before Einthoven was able to construct a reliable, practical system. The first EKG was introduced to the United States in 1909, and in 1924, Einthoven was awarded the Nobel Prize for physiology or medicine. Both Einthoven's system and the one used today are based on the fact that each time the heart beats, it produces electrical currents. It is these currents that actually make the heart contract or pump the blood that each cell in the body needs to stay alive and do its work.

In fact, every muscle and nerve cell is capable of producing a tiny electrical signal through a process called "depolarization." This means that in each cell, charged atomic particles called positive and negative ions are moving in and out of its membrane, and it is this movement that creates electrical currents. Therefore, an EKG is not a measurement of the heart's muscular activity but rather a measurement of the flow of ions (or the electrical current) through the membranes of the heart muscle before it contracts. Since a person's body is made up mainly of salty water, it is an excellent conductor of electricity and these currents can be detected at the surface of the skin.

Taking an EKG

Before an EKG is taken, electrodes or conducting plates are attached to the skin in certain areas. The electrodes are then connected by wires to a meter that boosts or amplifies the impulses, either recording them on a piece of paper using a pen attached to the meter or displaying them on some sort of monitor. During an EKG, a patient will usually have electrodes connected at both wrists and ankles as well as at six other points on the chest, roughly over the area of the heart. The electrodes are attached to the skin with sticky pads or suction cups. Sometimes a gel that helps conduction is applied to the skin before the electrodes are attached. Each of these electrode wires or "leads" is connected to the meter or the recording part of the EKG machine, and each wire registers a pattern of electrical impulses and displays it on a graph.

From the patient's point of view, he or she is usually lying down and is asked to remain still while the leads are attached as well as for the duration of the test. The entire recording is usually completed in five to ten minutes and requires nothing more of the patient. This test is painless, noninvasive, and it has no associated risks. There is absolutely no danger since the electricity involved comes from the patient's own heart, which then flows into the machine. No electricity ever passes from the machine into the patient. Whether recorded on a paper graph or on a monitor, the wavelike image produced is usually a small blip followed by a big blip. Although this pattern may look the same to the average person, the informed and trained eye of the professional can tell a great deal about the patient's heart according to how that pattern differs from the normal pattern.

Other types

Since doctors know that certain types of heart problems—like coronary artery blockage—do not show up on a resting EKG, they often prescribe a stress EKG to make sure that no condition goes undetected. For this test, the leads are attached the same way, but the patient is asked to exercise strenuously, usually on a treadmill machine. Since the heart requires a larger supply of blood while exercising, a stress EKG provides a more complete and accurate diagnosis than a resting EKG. Although patients usu-

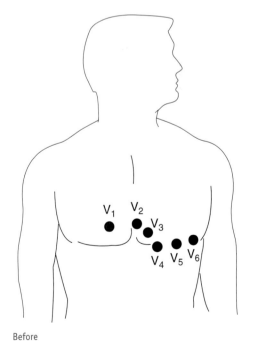

Before

ally have to go to a doctor's office for a stress EKG, resting EKG machines are small and portable and can be done in the home by a technician. EKG data can also be transmitted by using radiotelemetry techniques. Also called a transtelephonic EKG (pronounced tranz-tell-eh-FON-ik), this technology allows outpatient heart data to be transmitted to a hospital or wherever a doctor chooses.

Finally, EKGs can also be done continuously. In certain cases when a patient's heart problem arises only now and then, the doctor will request that a Holter monitor be worn while the patient goes about his or her normal day. This monitor has an amplifier and a cassette tape that

Electrocardiogram rhythm charts. *(Reproduced by permission of The Gale Group.)*

Normal Sinus Node Rhythm

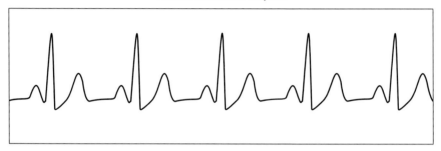

Respiratory Sinus Arrhythmia

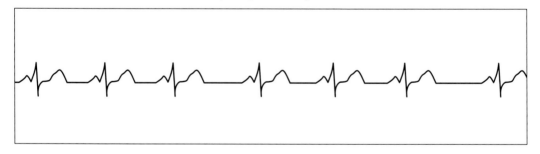

Ventricular Tachycardia

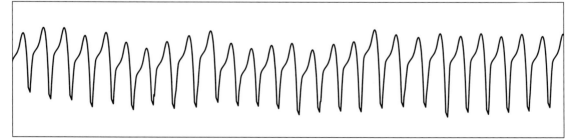

records the patient's EKG pattern. The monitor is sometimes worn for as long as forty-eight hours. The patient is also asked to keep track of any unusual activities or even emotional states that might affect his or her heart's rhythm.

[*See also* **Heart**]

Electrolysis

Electrolysis is a process by which electrical energy is used to produce a chemical change. Perhaps the most familiar example of electrolysis is the decomposition (breakdown) of water into hydrogen and oxygen by means of an electric current. The same process can be used to decompose compounds other than water. Sodium, chlorine, magnesium, and aluminum are four elements produced commercially by electrolysis.

Principles

The electrolysis of water illustrates the changes that take place when an electric current passes through a chemical compound. Water consists of water molecules, represented by the formula H_2O. In any sample of water, some small fraction of molecules exist in the form of ions, or charged particles. Ions are formed in water when water molecules break apart to form positively charged hydrogen ions and negatively charged hydroxide ions. Chemists describe that process with the following chemical equation:

$$H_2O \rightarrow H^+ + OH^-$$

In order for electrolysis to occur, ions must exist. Seawater can be electrolyzed, for example, because it contains many positively charged sodium ions (Na^+) and negatively charged chloride ions (Cl^-). Any liquid, like seawater, that contains ions is called an electrolyte.

Water is not usually considered an electrolyte because it contains so few hydrogen and hydroxide ions. Normally, only one water molecule out of two billion ionizes. In contrast, sodium chloride (table salt) breaks apart completely when dissolved in water. A salt water solution consists entirely of sodium ions and chloride ions.

In order to electrolyze water, then, one prior step is necessary. Some substance, similar to sodium chloride, must be added to water to make it an electrolyte. The substance that is usually used is sulfuric acid.

Words to Know

Anode: The electrode in an electrolytic cell through which electrons move from the electrolyte to the battery.

Cathode: The electrode in an electrolytic cell through which electrons move from the battery to the electrolyte.

Electrolyte: Any substance that, when dissolved in water, conducts an electric current.

Electrolytic cell: A system in which electrical energy is used to bring about chemical changes.

Electroplating: A process that uses an electrolytic cell to deposit a thin layer of metal on some kind of surface.

Ion: Any particle, such as an atom or molecule, that carries an electric charge.

The electrolysis process

The equipment used for electrolysis of a compound consists of three parts: a source of DC (direct) current; two electrodes; and an electrolyte. A common arrangement consists of a battery (the source of current) whose two poles are attached to two strips of platinum metal (the electrodes), which are immersed in water to which a few drops of sulfuric acid have been added (the electrolyte).

Electrolysis begins when electrical current (a flow of electrons) flows out of one pole of the battery into one electrode, the cathode. Positive hydrogen ions (H^+) in the electrolyte pick up electrons from that electrode and become neutral hydrogen molecules (H_2):

$$2\,H^+ + 2\,e^- \rightarrow H_2$$

(Hydrogen molecules are written as H_2 because they always occur as pairs of hydrogen atoms. The same is true for molecules of oxygen, O_2.)

As the electrolysis of water occurs, one can see tiny bubbles escaping from the electrolyte at the cathode. These are bubbles of hydrogen gas.

Bubbles can also be seen escaping from the second electrode, the anode. The anode is connected to the second pole of the battery, the pole through which electrons enter the battery. At this electrode, electrons are being taken out of the electrolyte and fed back into the battery. The electrons come from negatively charged hydroxide ions (OH⁻), which have an excess of electrons. The anode reaction is slightly more complicated than the cathode reaction, as shown by this chemical equation:

$$4 \, OH^- - 4 \, e^- \rightarrow O_2 + 2 \, H_2O$$

Essentially this equation says that electrons are taken away from hydroxide ions and oxygen gas is produced in the reaction. The oxygen gas bubbles off at the anode, while the extra water formed remains behind in the electrolyte.

The overall reaction that takes place in the electrolysis of water is now obvious. Electrons from the battery are given to hydrogen ions in the electrolyte, changing them into hydrogen gas. Electrons are taken from hydroxide ions in the electrolyte and transferred to the battery. Over time, water molecules are broken down to form hydrogen and oxygen molecules:

$$2 \, H_2O \rightarrow 2 \, H_2 + O_2$$

Commercial applications

Preparing elements.   Electrolysis is used to break down compounds that are very stable. For example, aluminum is a very important metal in modern society. It is used in everything from pots and pans to space shuttles. But the main natural source of aluminum, aluminum oxide, is a very stable compound. A compound that is stable is difficult to break apart. You can't get aluminum out of aluminum oxide just by heating the compound—you need more energy than heat can provide.

Aluminum is prepared by an electrolytic process first discovered in 1886 by a 21-year-old student at Oberlin College in Ohio, Charles Martin Hall (1863–1914). Hall found a way of melting aluminum oxide and then electrolyzing it. Once melted, aluminum oxide forms ions of aluminum and oxygen, which behave in much the same way as hydrogen and hydroxide ions in the previous example. Pure aluminum metal is obtained at the cathode, while oxygen gas bubbles off at the anode. Sodium, chlorine, and magnesium are three other elements obtained commercially by an electrolytic process similar to the Hall process.

Refining of copper.   Electrolysis can be used for purposes other than preparing elements. One example is the refining of copper. Very pure copper is often required in the manufacture of electrical equipment. (A purity of 99.999 percent is not unusual.) The easiest way to produce a product of this purity is with electrolysis.

An electrolytic cell for refining copper contains very pure copper at the cathode, impure copper at the anode, and copper sulfate as the electrolyte. When the anode and cathode are connected to a battery, electrons flow into the cathode, where they combine with copper ions (Cu^{2+}) in the electrolyte:

$$Cu^{2+} + 2\ e^- \rightarrow Cu^0$$

Pure copper metal (Cu^0 in the above equation) is formed on the cathode.

At the anode, copper atoms (Cu^0) lose electrons and become copper ions (Cu^{2+}) in the electrolyte:

$$Cu^0 - 2\ e^- \rightarrow Cu^{2+}$$

Overall, the only change that occurs in the cell is that copper atoms from the impure anode become copper ions in the electrolyte. Those copper ions are then plated out on the cathode. Any impurities in the anode are just left behind, and nearly 100 percent pure copper builds up on the cathode.

Electroplating. Another important use of electrolytic cells is in the electroplating of silver, gold, chromium, and nickel. Electroplating produces a very thin coating of these expensive metals on the surfaces of cheaper metals, giving them the appearance and the chemical resistance of the expensive ones.

In silver plating, the object to be plated (a spoon, for example) is used as the cathode. A bar of silver metal is used as the anode. And the electrolyte is a solution of silver cyanide (AgCN). When this arrangement is connected to a battery, electrons flow into the cathode where they combine with silver ions (Ag^+) from the electrolyte to form silver atoms (Ag^0):

$$Ag^+ + 1\ e^- \rightarrow Ag^0$$

These silver atoms plate out as a thin coating on the cathode—in this case, the spoon. At the anode, silver atoms give up electrons and become silver ions in the electrolyte:

$$Ag^0 - 1\ e^- \rightarrow Ag^0$$

Silver is cycled, therefore, from the anode to the electrolyte to the cathode, where it is plated out.

Electromagnetic field

An electromagnetic field is a region in space in which electric and magnetic forces interact. A magnetic compass will detect a magnetic field when held close to an electric wire carrying current to a lit lightbulb. The region around the wire has both electrical and magnetic properties and is, therefore, an electromagnetic field.

Electric fields and magnetic fields

At one time, scientists thought that electricity and magnetism were totally different forms of energy. The fact that a magnet can pick up certain kinds of materials was thought to have no connection with the flow of electrons through a wire. During the early 1800s, however, experiments began to disprove this view. The movement of electrons and magnetic poles are, as it turned out, closely related to each other.

In the simplest possible case, imagine a single charged particle, such as an electron, traveling through space at a constant speed and in a straight line. The electron creates an electric field around itself. An

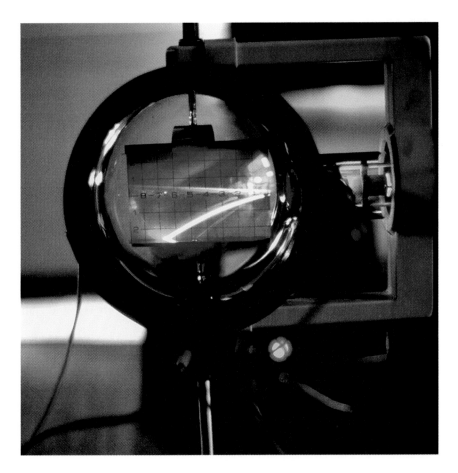

A demonstration of the effect of a magnetic field on an electron beam. *(Reproduced by permission of Photo Researchers, Inc.)*

electric field is a region in space in which a charged particle is affected. A second electron in the path of the first electron would be deflected by the movement of the first electron, that is, by the electric field created by the first electron.

But the moving electron also generates a magnetic field around itself. The field consists of circular lines of magnetic force around the electron's path. A tiny magnet placed near the electron's path would be twisted in one direction or another by this magnetic field.

The electromagnetic field surrounding the moving electron, then, is some combination of these electric and magnetic fields. That electromagnetic field can be expressed mathematically.

Maxwell's equations

Studying the nature of electromagnetic fields produced by changing electric currents is a more difficult task. The solution to such problems was first devised by English physicist James Clerk Maxwell (1831–1879). Maxwell discovered a set of mathematical equations that can be used to describe the combined electric and magnetic fields produced by a flow of charges.

Maxwell's discovery was one of the great achievements of nineteenth-century physics (the science of matter and energy). It demonstrated that electricity and magnetism are not totally distinct from each other but, instead, are closely related forms of energy. Maxwell's work was the first major step in a long-term effort by physicists to show how all forms of energy are related to each other.

Maxwell's equations are also important because they apply to such a vast range of phenomena. Cosmic rays, X rays, ultraviolet light, infrared radiation, visible light, radar, radio waves, and microwaves may appear to be very different from each other. Yet, they are all forms of energy with which electromagnetic fields are associated. They can all be understood through the use of Maxwell's equations.

Electromagnetic induction

The term electromagnetic induction refers to the generation of an electric current by passing a metal wire through a magnetic field. The discovery of electromagnetic induction in 1831 was preceded a decade earlier by a related discovery by Danish physicist Hans Christian Oersted (1777–

▼ **Words to Know**

Electric current: A flow of electrons.

Electrical generator: A device for converting mechanical (kinetic) energy into electrical energy.

Galvanometer: An instrument used to measure the flow of electric current.

Potential difference: Also called voltage; the amount of electric energy stored in a mass of electric charges compared to the energy stored in some other mass of charges.

Transformer: A device that transfers electric energy from one circuit to another circuit with different characteristics.

1851). Oersted showed that an electric current produces a magnetic field. That is, if you place a simple magnetic compass near any of the electrical wires in your home that are carrying a current, you can detect a magnetic field around the wires. If an electric current can produce a magnetic field, physicists reasoned, perhaps the reverse effect could be observed as well. So they set out to generate an electric current from a magnetic field.

That effect was first observed in 1831 by English physicist Michael Faraday (1791–1867) and shortly thereafter by American physicist Joseph Henry (1797–1878). The principle on which the Faraday-Henry discovery is based is shown in the figure on page 762. A long piece of metal wire is wound around a metal bar. The two ends of the wire are connected to a galvanometer, an instrument used to measure electric current. The bar is then placed between the poles of a magnet.

As long as the bar remains at rest, nothing happens. No current is generated. But moving the bar in one direction or another produces a current that can be read on the galvanometer. When the bar is moved downward, current flows in one direction through the metal wire. When the bar is moved upward, current flows in the opposite direction through the wire. The amount of current that flows is proportional to the speed with which the wire moves through the magnetic field. When the wire moves faster, a larger current is produced. When it moves more slowly, a smaller current is produced.

Actually, it is not necessary to move the wire in order to produce the electric current. One could just as well hold the wire still and move the magnetic poles. All that is necessary is the creation of some relative motion of the wire and the magnetic field. When that happens, an electric current is generated.

Applications

Many electrical devices operate on the principle of electromagnetic induction. Perhaps the most important of these is an electrical generator. An electrical generator is a device for converting kinetic energy (the energy of an object due to its motion) into electrical energy. In a generator, a wire coil is placed between the poles of a magnet and caused to spin at a high rate of speed. One way to make the coil spin is to attach it to a turbine powered by water, as in a dam. Steam from a boiler can also be used to make the coil spin.

As the coil spins between the poles of the magnet, an electric current is generated. That current then can be sent out along transmission lines to homes, office buildings, factories, and other consumers of electric power.

Transformers also operate on the principle of electromagnetic induction. Transformers are devices that convert electric current from one potential difference (voltage) to another potential difference. For exam-

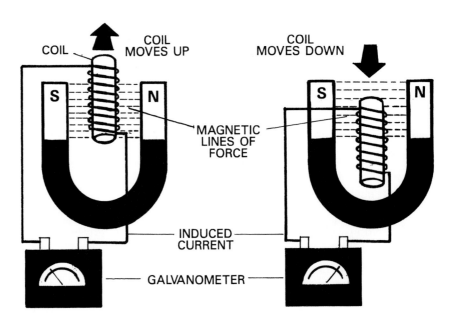

A figure of electromagnetic induction. (Reproduced by permission of The Gale Group.)

ple, the current that comes from a power plant is typically high voltage current, much higher than is needed or than can be used in household appliances. A step-down transformer uses electromagnetic induction to convert the high voltage current in power lines to the lower voltage current needed for household appliances.

[*See also* **Electric current; Electromagnetic field; Generator; Transformer**]

Electromagnetic spectrum

The term electromagnetic spectrum refers to all forms of energy transmitted by means of waves traveling at the speed of light. Visible light is a form of electromagnetic radiation, but the term also applies to cosmic rays, X rays, ultraviolet radiation, infrared radiation, radio waves, radar, and microwaves. These forms of electromagnetic radiation make up the electromagnetic spectrum much as the various colors of light make up the visible spectrum (the rainbow).

Wavelength and frequency

Any wave—including an electromagnetic wave—can be described by two properties: its wavelength and frequency. The wavelength of a wave is the distance between two successive identical parts of the wave, as between two wave peaks or crests. The Greek letter lambda (λ) is often used to represent wavelength. Wavelength is measured in various units, depending on the kind of wave being discussed. For visible light, for example, wavelength is often expressed in nanometers (billionths of a meter); for radio waves, wavelengths are usually expressed in centimeters or meters.

Frequency is the rate at which waves pass a given point. The frequency of an X-ray beam, for example, might be expressed as 10^{18} hertz. The term hertz (abbreviation: Hz) is a measure of the number of waves that pass a given point per second of time. If you could watch the X-ray beam from some given position, you would see 1,000,000,000,000,000,000 (that is, 10^{18}) wave crests pass you every second.

For every electromagnetic wave, the product of the wavelength and frequency equals a constant, the speed of light (c). In other words, $\lambda \cdot f = c$. This equation shows that wavelength and frequency have a reciprocal relationship to each other. As one increases, the other must

Words to Know

Electromagnetic radiation: Radiation that travels through a vacuum with the speed of light and that has properties of both an electric and magnetic wave.

Frequency: The number of waves that pass a given point in a given period of time.

Hertz: The unit of frequency; a measure of the number of waves that pass a given point per second of time.

Wavelength: The distance between two successive peaks or crests in a wave.

decrease. Gamma rays, for example, have very small wavelengths and very large frequencies. Radio waves, by contrast, have large wavelengths and very small frequencies.

Regions of the electromagnetic spectrum

As shown in the accompanying figure, the whole range of the electromagnetic spectrum can be divided up into various regions based on wavelength and frequency. Electromagnetic radiation with very short wavelengths and high frequencies fall into the cosmic ray/gamma ray/ ultraviolet radiation region. At the other end of the spectrum are the long wavelength, low frequency forms of radiation: radio, radar, and microwaves. In the middle of the range is visible light.

Properties of waves in different regions of the spectrum are commonly described by different notation. Visible radiation is usually described by its wavelength, while X rays are described by their energy. All of these schemes are equivalent, however; they are just different ways of describing the same properties.

The boundaries between types of electromagnetic radiation are rather loose. Thus, a wave with a frequency of 8×10^{14} hertz could be described as a form of very deep violet visible light or as a form of ultraviolet radiation.

Applications

The various forms of electromagnetic radiation are used everywhere in the world around us. Radio waves are familiar to us because of their use in communications. The standard AM radio band includes radiation in the 540 to 1650 kilohertz (thousands of hertz) range. The FM band includes the 88 to 108 megahertz (millions of hertz) range. This region also includes shortwave radio transmissions and television broadcasts.

Microwaves are probably most familiar to people because of microwave ovens. In a microwave oven, food is heated when microwaves excite water molecules contained within foods (and the molecules' motion produces heat). In astronomy, emission of radiation at a wavelength of 8 inches (21 centimeters) has been used to identify neutral hydrogen throughout the galaxy. Radar is also included in this region.

The infrared region of the spectrum is best known to us because of the fact that heat is a form of infrared radiation. But the visible wavelength range is the range of frequencies with which we are most familiar. These are the wavelengths to which the human eye is sensitive and which most easily pass through Earth's atmosphere. This region is further broken down into the familiar colors of the rainbow, also known as the visible spectrum.

The ultraviolet range lies at wavelengths just short of the visible range. Most of the ultraviolet radiation reaching Earth in sunlight is absorbed in the upper atmosphere. Ozone, a form of oxygen, has the ability to trap ultraviolet radiation and prevent it from reaching Earth. This fact is important since ultraviolet radiation can cause a number of problems for both plants and animals. The depletion of the ozone layer during the 1970s and 1980s was a matter of some concern to scientists because of the increase in dangerous ultraviolet radiation reaching Earth.

We are most familiar with X rays because of their uses in medicine. X-radiation can pass through soft tissue in the body, allowing doctors to examine bones and teeth from the outside. Since X rays do not penetrate Earth's atmosphere, astronomers must place X-ray telescopes in space.

Gamma rays are the most energetic of all electromagnetic radiation, and we have little experience with them in everyday life. They are produced by nuclear processes—during radioactive decay (in which an element gives off energy by the disintegration of its nucleus) or in nuclear reactions in stars or in space.

[*See also* **Frequency; Light; X rays**]

Electromagnetism

Electromagnetism is the force involving the interaction of electricity and magnetism. It is the science of electrical charge, and its rules govern the way charged particles of atoms interact. Electromagnetism is one of the four fundamental forces of the universe (gravity and the "strong" and "weak" forces that hold an atomic nucleus together are the other three). Because its effects can be observed so easily, electromagnetism is the best understood of these four forces.

Some of the rules of electrostatics, or the study of electric charges at rest, were first noted by the ancient Romans, who observed the way a brushed comb would attract particles. Until the nineteenth century, however, electricity and magnetism were thought to be totally different and separate forces. In 1820, a direct connection between the two forces was confirmed for the first time when Danish physicist Hans Christian Oersted (1777–1851) announced his discovery that an electric current, if passed through a wire placed near a compass needle, would make the needle move. This suggested that electricity somehow creates a magnetic force or field, since a compass needle moves by magnetism.

Shortly afterward, French physicist André Marie Ampère (1775–1836) conducted experiments in which he discovered that two parallel

A MAGLEV supertrain.
(Reproduced by permission of Phototake.)

▼ Words to Know

Electromagnetic radiation: Radiation (a form of energy) that has properties of both an electric and magnetic wave and that travels through a vacuum with the speed of light.

Electromagnetic spectrum: The complete array of electromagnetic radiation, including radio waves (at the longest-wavelength end), microwaves, infrared radiation, visible light, ultraviolet radiation, X rays, and gamma rays (at the shortest-wavelength end).

Frequency: The rate at which vibrations take place (number of times per second the motion is repeated), given in cycles per second or in hertz (Hz). Also, the number of waves that pass a given point in a given period of time.

wires each carrying a current attract each other if the currents flow in the same direction, but repel each other if they flow in opposite directions. He concluded that magnetism is the result of electricity in motion.

A decade after Oersted's experiments, English physicist Michael Faraday (1791–1867) observed that an electric current flowing in a wire created what he called "lines of force" to expand outward, inducing or causing an electric flow in a crossed wire. Since it was known from Oersted's work that an electric current always produces a magnetic field around itself, Faraday concluded from his experiments just the opposite: that a wire moving through a magnetic field will induce an electric current in the wire.

Finally, between 1864 and 1873, Scottish physicist James Clerk Maxwell (1831–1879) devised a set of mathematical equations that unified electrical and magnetic phenomena into what became known as the electromagnetic theory. He and his contemporaries now understood that an electric current creates a magnetic field around it. If the motion of that current changes, then the magnetic field varies, which in turn produces an electric field.

Maxwell also discovered that the oscillation or fluctuation of an electric current would produce a magnetic field that expanded outward at a constant speed. By applying the ratio of the units of magnetic phenomena to the units of electrical phenomena, he found it possible to calculate the speed of that expansion. The calculation came out to approximately

186,300 miles (300,000 kilometers) per second, nearly the speed of light. From this, Maxwell theorized that light itself was a form of electromagnetic radiation that traveled in waves. Since electric charges could be made to oscillate at many velocities (speeds), there should be a corresponding number of electromagnetic radiations. Therefore, visible light would be just a small part of the electromagnetic spectrum, or the complete array of electromagnetic radiation.

Indeed, modern scientists know that radio and television waves, microwaves, infrared rays, ultraviolet light, visible light, gamma rays, and X rays are all electromagnetic waves that travel through space independent of matter. And they all travel at roughly the same speed—the speed of light—differing from each other only in the frequency at which their electric and magnetic fields oscillate.

Many common events depend upon the broad span of the electromagnetic spectrum. The ability to communicate across long distances despite intervening obstacles, such as the walls of buildings, is possible using the radio and television frequencies. X rays can see into the human body without opening it. These things, which would once have been labeled magic, are now ordinary ways we use the electromagnetic spectrum.

The unification of electricity and magnetism has led to a deeper understanding of physical science, and much effort has been put into further unifying the four forces of nature. Scientists have demonstrated that the weak force and electromagnetism are part of the same fundamental force, which they call the electroweak force. There are proposals to include the strong force in a grand unified theory, which attempts to show how the four forces can be thought of as a manifestation of a single basic force that broke apart when the universe cooled after the big bang (theory that explains the beginning of the universe as a tremendous explosion from a single point that occurred 12 to 15 billion years ago). The inclusion of gravity in the unified theory, however, remains an open problem for scientists.

[*See also* **Electricity; Electromagnetic field; Electromagnetic induction; Magnetism**]

Electron

The electron is a subatomic (smaller than an atom) particle that carries a single unit of negative electricity. All matter consists of atoms that, in turn, contain three very small particles: protons, neutrons, and electrons.

Words to Know

Electric current: A flow of electrons.

Energy level: A region of the atom in which there is a high probability of finding electrons.

Nucleus (atomic): The central core of an atom, consisting of protons and (usually) neutrons.

Positron: The antiparticle of the electron. It has the same mass and spin as the electron, but its charge, though equal in magnitude, is opposite in sign to that of the electron.

Of these three, only electrons are thought to be fundamental particles, that is, incapable of being broken down into simpler particles.

The presence or absence of an excess of electrons is responsible for all electrical phenomena. Suppose a metal wire is connected to two ends of a battery. Electrical pressure from electrons within the battery force electrons in atoms of the metal to flow. That flow of electrons is an electric current.

Electron energy levels

The protons and neutrons in an atom are packed together in a central core known as the nucleus of the atom. The size of the nucleus is many thousands of times smaller than the size of the atom itself. Electrons are distributed in specific regions outside the nucleus. At one time, scientists thought that electrons traveled in very specific pathways around the nucleus, similar to the orbits traveled by planets in the solar system.

But it is known that the orbit concept is not appropriate for electrons. The uncertainty principle, a fundamental law of physics (the science of matter and energy), says that the pathway traveled by very small particles like an electron can never be defined perfectly. Instead, scientists now talk about the *probability* of finding an electron in an atom. In some regions of the atom, that probability is very high (although never 100 percent), and in other regions it is very low (but never 0 percent). The regions in space where the probability of finding an electron is high corresponds roughly to the orbits about which scientists talked earlier. Those regions are now called energy levels.

Electron properties

Electrons have three fundamental properties: charge, mass, and spin. By definition, the electric charge on an electron is -1. The mass of an electron has been measured and found to be 9.109389×10^{-31} kilograms. Electrons also spin on their axes in much the same way that planets do. Spinning electrons, like any other moving electric charge, create a magnetic field around themselves. That magnetic field affects the way electrons arrange themselves in atoms and how they react with each other. The field is also responsible for the magnetic properties of materials.

History

During the nineteenth century, scientists made a number of important basic discoveries about electrical phenomena. However, no one could explain the fundamental nature of electricity itself. Then, in 1897, English physicist J. J. Thomson (1856–1940) discovered the electron. He was able to show that a flow of electric current consisted of individual particles, all of which had exactly the same ratio of electric charge to mass (e/m). He obtained the same result using a number of different materials and concluded that these particles are present in all forms of matter. The name given to these particles—electrons—had actually been

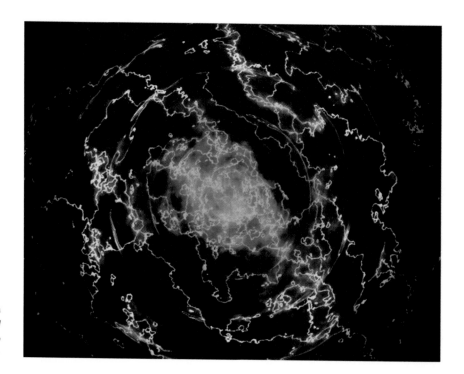

The electrondensity of a helium atom. *(Reproduced by permission of Photo Researchers, Inc.)*

suggested some years earlier by Irish physicist George Johnstone Stoney (1826–1911).

Although Thomson was able to measure the ratio of electric charge of mass (e/m) for an electron, he did not know how to determine either of these two quantities individually. That problem puzzled physicists for more than a decade. Finally, the riddle was solved by American physicist Robert Andrew Millikan (1868–1953) in a series of experiments conducted between 1907 and 1913. The accompanying figure outlines the main features of Millikan's famous oil drop experiment.

The oil drops needed for the experiment are produced by a common squeeze-bulb atomizer. The tiny droplets formed by this method fall downward and through the hole in the upper plate under the influence of gravity. As they fall, the droplets are given a negative electric charge.

Once droplets enter the space between the two plates, the high-voltage source is turned on. The negatively charged oil droplets are then attracted upward by the positive charge on the upper metal plate. At this point, the droplets are being tugged by two opposite forces: gravity, pulling them downward, and an electrical force, pulling them upward.

By carefully adjusting the voltage used, Millikan was able to keep oil droplets suspended in space between the two plates. Since the droplets moved neither upward or downward, he knew that the gravitational force on the droplets was exactly matched by the electric force. From this information, he was able to calculate the value of the electric charge on a droplet. The result he obtained, a charge of 1.591×10^{-10} coulomb, is

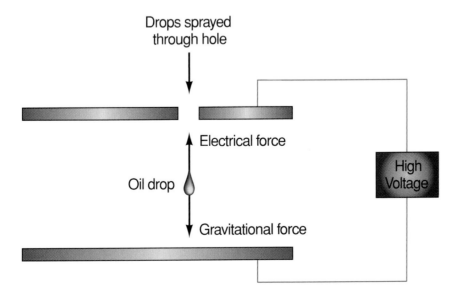

Drops sprayed through hole

Electrical force

Oil drop

Gravitational force

High Voltage

A figure outlining the main features of Millikan's oil drop experiment. *(Reproduced by permission of The Gale Group.)*

Quantum Number

How would you send a letter to an electron? As strange as that question seems, electrons have "addresses," just as people do.

Think of an oxygen atom, for example. Every oxygen atom has eight electrons. But those eight electrons are all different from each other. The differences among the eight electrons are represented by quantum numbers. A quantum number is a number that describes some physical property of an object (in this case, of an electron).

We know that any electron can be completely described by stating four of its properties. Those properties are represented by four different quantum numbers represented by the letters n, ℓ, m_ℓ, and s. Quantum number n, for example, represents the distance of an electron from the nucleus. Any electron for which $n = 1$ is in the first orbit around the nucleus of the atom. Quantum number ℓ represents the shape of the electron's orbit, that is, how flattened out its orbit is. Quantum number m_ℓ represents the magnetic properties of the electron. And quantum number s represents the spin of the electron, whether it's spinning in a clockwise or counter-clockwise direction.

So if you decide to send a letter to electron X, whose quantum numbers are 3, 2, 0, $+\frac{1}{2}$, you know it will go to an electron in the third orbit, with a flattened orbital path, certain magnetic properties, and a clockwise spin.

very close to the value accepted today of 1.602177×10^{-19} coulomb. (The coulomb is the standard metric unit of electrical charge.)

The positron

One of the interesting detective stories in science involves the discovery of an electron-type particle called the positron. During the 1920s, English physicist Paul Dirac (1902–1984) was using the new tools of quantum mechanics to analyze the nature of matter. Some of the equations he solved had negative answers. Those answers troubled him since he was not sure what a negative answer—the opposite of some property— could mean. One way he went about explaining these answers was to hypothesize the existence of a twin of the electron. The twin would have every property of the electron itself, Dirac said, except for one: it would carry a single unit of positive electricity rather than a single unit of negative electricity.

Dirac's prediction was confirmed only two years after he announced his hypothesis. American physicist Carl David Anderson (1905–1991) found positively charged electrons in a cosmic ray shower that he was studying. Anderson called these particles positrons, for *posi*tive elec*trons*. Today, scientists understand that positrons are only one form of antimatter, particles similar to fundamental particles such as the proton, neutron, and electron, but with one property opposite to that of the fundamental particle.

[*See also* **Antiparticle; Quantum mechanics; Subatomic particles**]

Electronics

Electronics is the branch of physics (the science of matter and energy) that deals with the flow of electrons and other carriers of electric charge. This flow of electric charge is known as electric current, and a closed path through which current travels is called an electric circuit.

An electronic microprocessor used to operate an elevator. *(Reproduced by permission of The Stock Market.)*

The modern era of electronics originated in the early twentieth century with the invention of the electron tube. An electron tube is a device that stores electric charges and amplifies (intensifies or strengthens) electronic signals. In 1947 the industry took a giant leap forward when American physicists John Bardeen (1908–1991), Walter Brattain (1902–1987), and William Shockley (1910–1989) developed the smaller, more efficient transistor, which led to a new generation of miniature electronics. In the late 1950s, American physicist Robert Noyce (1927–1990) invented the silicon integrated circuit—an even more efficient way to process electronic impulses that has carried the electronics industry into the computer age. The 1980s saw the development of circuits employing very-large-scale integration (VLSI). VLSI technology involves placement of 100,000 or more transistors on a single silicon chip. VLSI greatly expands the computational speed and ability of computers. Microcomputers, medical equipment, video cameras, and communication satellites are just a few examples of devices made possible by integrated circuits. Researchers believe that, in the future, new technologies may make it possible to fit one billion or more transistors on a single chip.

Of the many forms of electronics, none has helped transform our lives more than digital electronics, which began in the 1970s. The personal computer is one of the best examples of this transformation because it has simplified tasks that were difficult or impossible for individuals to complete.

Today electronics has a vast array of applications including television, computers, microwave ovens, radar, radio, sound recording and reproduction equipment, video technology, and X-ray tubes.

[*See also* **Electric current; Transistor; Vacuum tube**]

Element, chemical

A chemical element can be defined in one of two ways: experimentally or theoretically. Experimentally, an element is any substance that cannot be broken down into any simpler substance. Imagine that you are given a piece of pure iron and asked to break it down using any device or method ever invented by chemists. Nothing you can do will ever change the iron into anything simpler. Iron, therefore, is an element.

The experimental definition of an element can be explained by using a second definition: an element is a substance in which all atoms are of the same kind. If there were a way to look at each of the individual atoms in the bar of pure iron mentioned above, they would all be the

↓ Words to Know

Atomic mass: The mass of the protons, neutrons, and electrons that make up an atom.

Atomic number: The number of protons in the nucleus of an element's atom.

Chemical symbol: A letter or pair of letters that represents some given amount of an element.

Compound, chemical: A substance that consists of two or more chemical elements joined to each other in a specific proportion.

Metal: An element that loses electrons in chemical reactions with other elements.

Metalloid: An element that acts sometimes like a metal and sometimes like a nonmetal.

Nonmetal: An element that tends to gain electrons in chemical reactions with other elements.

Periodic table: A system of classifying the chemical elements according to their atomic number.

Synthetic element: An element that is made artificially in a laboratory but is generally not found in nature.

same—all atoms of iron. In contrast, a chemical compound, such as iron oxide, always contains at least two different kinds of atoms, in this case, atoms of iron and atoms of oxygen.

Natural and synthetic elements

Ninety-two chemical elements occur naturally on Earth. The others have been made synthetically or artificially in a laboratory. Synthetic elements are usually produced in particle accelerators (devices used to increase the velocity of subatomic particles such as electrons and protons) or nuclear reactors (devices used to control the energy released by nuclear reactions). The first synthetic element to be produced was technetium, discovered in 1937 by Italian American physicist Emilio Segrè (1905–1989) and his colleague C. Perrier. Except for technetium and promethium, all synthetic elements have larger nuclei than uranium.

Two Dozen Common and Important Chemical Elements

| Element | Symbol | Percent of all atoms* | | | | Characteristics under ordinary room conditions |
		In the universe	In Earth's crust	In sea water	In the human body	
Aluminum	Al	—	6.3	—	—	A lightweight, silvery metal
Calcium	Ca	—	2.1	—	.02	Common in minerals, seashells, and bones
Carbon	C	—	—	—	10.7	Basic in all living things
Chlorine	Cl	—	—	0.3	—	A toxic gas
Copper	Cu	—	—	—	—	The only red metal
Gold	Au	—	—	—	—	The only yellow metal
Helium	He	7.1	—	—	—	A very light gas
Hydrogen	H	92.8	2.9	66.2	60.6	The lightest of all elements; a gas
Iodine	I	—	—	—	—	A nonmetal; used as antiseptic
Iron	Fe	—	2.1	—	—	A magnetic metal; used in steel
Lead	Pb	—	—	—	—	A soft, heavy metal
Magnesium	Mg	—	2.0	—	—	A very light metal
Mercury	Hg	—	—	—	—	A liquid metal; one of the two liquid elements
Nickel	Ni	—	—	—	—	A noncorroding metal; used in coins
Nitrogen	N	—	—	—	2.4	A gas; the major component of air
Oxygen	O	—	60.1	33.1	25.7	A gas; the second major component of air
Phosphorus	P	—	—	—	0.1	A nonmetal; essential to plants
Potassium	K	—	1.1	—	—	A metal; essential to plants; commonly called "potash"
Silicon	Si	—	20.8	—	—	A semiconductor; used in electronics
Silver	Ag	—	—	—	—	A very shiny, valuable metal
Sodium	Na	—	2.2	0.3	—	A soft metal; reacts readily with water, air
Sulfur	S	—	—	—	0.1	A yellow nonmetal; flammable
Titanium	Ti	—	0.3	—	—	A light, strong, noncorroding metal used in space vehicles
Uranium	U	—	—	—	—	A very heavy metal; fuel for nuclear power

*If no number is entered, the element constitutes less than 0.1 percent.

At the beginning of the twenty-first century, there were 114 known elements, ranging from hydrogen (H), whose atoms have only one electron, to the as-yet unnamed element whose atoms contain 114 electrons. New elements are difficult to produce. Only a few atoms can be made at a time, and it usually takes years before scientists agree on who discovered what and when.

Classifying elements

More than 100 years ago, chemists began searching for ways to organize the chemical elements. At first, they tried listing them by the size (mass) of their nucleus, their atomic mass. Later, they found that using the number of protons in their atomic nuclei was a more effective technique. They invented a property known as atomic number for this organization. The atomic number of an element is defined as the number of protons in the nucleus of an atom of that element. Hydrogen has an atomic number of 1, for example, because the nuclei of hydrogen atoms each contain one—and only one—proton. Similarly, oxygen has an atomic number of 8 because the nuclei of all oxygen atoms contain 8 protons. The accompanying table (periodic table of the elements) contains a list of the known chemical elements arranged in order according to their atomic number.

Notice that the chemical symbol for each element is also included in the table. The chemical symbol of an element is a letter or pair of letters that stands for some given amount of the element, for example, for one atom of the element. Thus, the symbol Ca stands for one atom of calcium, and the symbol W stands for one atom of tungsten. Chemical symbols, therefore, are not really abbreviations.

Chemical elements can be fully identified, therefore, by any one of three characteristics: their name, their chemical symbol, or their atomic number. If you know any one of these identifiers, you immediately know the other two. Saying "Na" to a chemist immediately tells that person that you are referring to sodium, element #11. Similarly, if you say "element 19," the chemist knows that you're referring to potassium, known by the symbol K.

The system of classifying elements used by chemists today is called the periodic table. The law on which the periodic table is based was first discovered almost simultaneously by German chemist Julius Lothar Meyer (1830–1895) and Russian chemist Dmitry Mendeleev (1834–1907) in about 1870. The periodic table is one of the most powerful tools in chemistry because it organizes the chemical elements in groups that have similar physical and chemical properties.

Main-Group Elements

Main-Group Elements

Transition Metals

Inner-Transition Metals

Atomic number 86 (222) **Atomic weight**
Symbol Rn
Name radon

1 IA																	18 VIIIA
1 1.00794 H hyd	2 IIA											13 IIIA	14 IVA	15 VA	16 VIA	17 VIIA	2 4.002602 He helium
3 6.941 Li lithium	4 9.012182 Be beryllium											5 10.811 B boron	6 12.011 C carbon	7 14.00674 N nitrogen	8 15.9994 O oxygen	9 18.9984032 F fluorine	10 20.1797 Ne neon
11 22.989768 Na sodium	12 24.3050 Mg magnesium	3 IIIB	4 IVB	5 VB	6 VIB	7 VIIB	8	9 VIIIB	10	11 IB	12 IIB	13 26.981539 Al aluminum	14 28.0855 Si silicon	15 30.973762 P phosphorus	16 32.066 S sulfur	17 35.4527 Cl chlorine	18 39.948 Ar argon
19 39.0983 K potassium	20 40.078 Ca calcium	21 44.955910 Sc scandium	22 47.88 Ti titanium	23 50.9415 V vanadium	24 51.9961 Cr chromium	25 54.9305 Mn manganese	26 55.847 Fe iron	27 58.93320 Co cobalt	28 58.69 Ni nickel	29 63.546 Cu copper	30 65.39 Zn zinc	31 69.723 Ga gallium	32 72.61 Ge germanium	33 74.92159 As arsenic	34 78.96 Se selenium	35 79.904 Br bromine	36 83.80 Kr krypton
37 85.4678 Rb rubidium	38 87.62 Sr strontium	39 88.90585 Y yttrium	40 91.224 Zr zirconium	41 92.90638 Nb niobium	42 95.94 Mo molybdenum	43 (98) Tc technetium	44 101.07 Ru ruthenium	45 102.90550 Rh rhodium	46 106.42 Pd palladium	47 107.8682 Ag silver	48 112.411 Cd cadmium	49 114.82 In indium	50 118.710 Sn tin	51 121.75 Sb antimony	52 127.60 Te tellurium	53 126.90447 I iodine	54 131.29 Xe xenon
55 132.90543 Cs cesium	56 137.327 Ba barium	57 138.9055 *La lanthanum	72 178.49 Hf hafnium	73 180.9479 Ta tantalum	74 183.85 W tungsten	75 186.207 Re rhenium	76 190.2 Os osmium	77 192.22 Ir iridium	78 195.08 Pt platinum	79 196.96654 Au gold	80 200.59 Hg mercury	81 204.3833 Tl thallium	82 207.2 Pb lead	83 208.98037 Bi bismuth	84 (209) Po polonium	85 (210) At astatine	86 (222) Rn radon
87 (223) Fr francium	88 (226) Ra radium	89 (227) †Ac actinium	104 (261) Unq unnilquadium	105 (262) Unp unnilpentium	106 (263) Unh unnilhexium	107 (262) Uns unnilseptium	108 (265) Uno unniloctium	109 (267) Une unnilennium									

Period 1 2 3 4 5 6 7

*Lanthanides	58 140.115 Ce cerium	59 140.90765 Pr praseodymium	60 144.24 Nd neodymium	61 (145) Pm promethium	62 150.36 Sm samarium	63 151.965 Eu europium	64 157.25 Gd gadolinium	65 158.92534 Tb terbium	66 162.50 Dy dysprosium	67 164.93032 Ho holmium	68 167.26 Er erbium	69 168.93421 Tm thulium	70 173.04 Yb ytterbium	71 174.967 Lu lutehium
†Actinides	90 232.0381 Th thorium	91 (231) Pa protactinium	92 238.0289 U uranium	93 (237) Np neptunium	94 (244) Pu plutonium	95 (243) Am americium	96 (247) Cm curium	97 (247) Bk berkelium	98 (251) Cf californium	99 (252) Es einsteinium	100 (257) Fm fermium	101 (258) Md mendelevium	102 (259) No nobelium	103 (262) Lr lowrencium

Periodic table of the elements. *(Reproduced by permission of The Gale Group.)*

A Who's Who of the Elements

Element	Distinction	Comment
Astatine (At)	The rarest	Rarest of the naturally occurring elements
Boron (B)	The strongest	Highest stretch resistance
Californium (Cf)	The most expensive	Sold at one time for about $1 billion a gram
Carbon (C)	The hardest	As diamond, one of its three solid forms
Germanium (Ge)	The purest	Has been purified to 99.99999999 percent purity
Helium (He)	The lowest melting point	–271.72°C at a pressure of 26 times atmospheric pressure
Hydrogen (H)	The lowest density	Density 0.0000899 g/cc at atmospheric pressure and 0°C
Lithium (Li)	The lowest–density metal	Density 0.534g/cc
Osmium (Os)	The highest density	Density 22.57 g/cc
Radon (Rn)	The highest–density gas	Density 0.00973 g/cc at atmospheric pressure and 0°C
Tungsten (W)	The highest melting point	3,420°C

Properties of the elements

One useful way of describing the chemical elements is according to their metallic or nonmetallic character. Most metals are hard with bright, shiny surfaces, often white or grey in color. Since important exceptions to this rule exist, metals are more properly defined according to the way they behave in chemical reactions. Metals, by this definition, are elements that lose electrons to other elements. By comparison, nonmetals are elements that gain electrons from other elements in chemical reactions. (They may be gases, liquids, or solids but seldom look like a metal.) The vast majority (93) of the elements are metals; the rest are nonmetals.

Historical background

The concept of a chemical element goes back more than 2,000 years. Ancient Greek philosophers conceived of the idea that some materials are more fundamental, or basic, than others. They listed obviously important

Formation of the Elements

How were the chemical elements formed? Scientists believe the answer to that question lies in the stars and in the processes by which stars are formed. The universe is thought to have been created at some moment in time 12 to 15 billion years ago. Prior to that moment, nothing other than energy is thought to have existed. But something occurred to transform that energy into an enormous explosion: the big bang. In the seconds following the big bang, matter began to form.

According to the big bang theory, the simplest forms of matter to appear were protons and electrons. Some of these protons and electrons combined to form atoms of hydrogen. A hydrogen atom consists of one proton and one electron; it is the simplest atom that can exist. Slowly, over long periods of time, hydrogen atoms began to come together in regions of space forming dense clouds. The hydrogen in these clouds was pulled closer and closer together by gravitational forces. Eventually these clouds of hydrogen were dense enough to form stars.

A star is simply a mass of matter that generates energy by nuclear reactions. The most common of these reactions involves the

materials such as earth, air, fire, and water as possibly being such "elemental" materials. These speculations belonged in the category of philosophy, however, rather than science. The Greeks had no way of testing their ideas to confirm them.

In fact, a few elements were already known long before the speculations of the Greek philosophers. No one at that time called these materials elements or thought of them as being different from the materials we call compounds today. Among the early elements used by humans were iron, copper, silver, tin, and lead. We know that early civilizations knew about and used these elements because of tools, weapons, and pieces of art that remain from the early periods of human history.

Another group of elements was discovered by the alchemists, the semi-mystical scholars who contributed to the early development of chemistry. These elements include antimony, arsenic, bismuth, phosphorus, and zinc.

The modern definition of an element was first provided by English chemist Robert Boyle (1627–1691). Boyle defined elements as "certain

combination of four hydrogen atoms to make one helium atom. As soon as stars began to form, then, helium became the second element found in the universe.

As stars grow older, they switch from hydrogen-to-helium nuclear reactions to other nuclear reactions. In another such reaction, helium atoms combine to form carbon atoms. Later carbon atoms combine to form oxygen, neon, sodium, and magnesium. Still later, neon and oxygen combine with each other to form magnesium. As these reactions continue, more and more of the chemical elements are formed.

At some point, all stars die. The nuclear reactions on which they depend for their energy come to an end. In some cases, a star's death is dramatic. It may actually blow itself apart, like an atomic bomb. The elements of which the star was made are then spread throughout the universe. They remain in space until they are drawn into the core of other stars or other astronomical bodies, such as our own Earth. If this theory is correct, then the atoms of iron, silver, and oxygen you see around you every day actually started out life in the middle of a star billions of miles away.

primitive and simple, or perfectly unmingled bodies; which not being made of any other bodies, or of one another, are the ingredients of which all those call'd perfectly mixed bodies are immediately compounded, and into which they are ultimately resolved." For all practical purposes, Boyle's definition of an element has remained the standard working definition for a chemical element ever since.

By the year 1800, no more than about 25 true elements had been discovered. During the next hundred years, however, that situation changed rapidly. By the end of the century, 80 elements were known. The rapid pace of discovery during the 1800s can be attributed to the development of chemistry as a science, to the improved tools of analysis available to chemists, and to the new predictive power provided by the periodic law of 1870.

During the twentieth century, the last remaining handful of naturally occurring elements were discovered and the synthetic elements were first manufactured.

El Niño

El Niño (pronounced el-NEEN-yo) is the name given to a change in the flow of water currents in the Pacific Ocean near the equator. El Niño—Spanish for "the child" because it often occurs around Christmas—repeats every three to five years. Although El Niño takes place in a small portion of the Pacific, it can affect the weather in large parts of Asia, Africa, Indonesia, and North and South America. Scientists have only recently become aware of the far-reaching effects of this phenomenon.

What is El Niño?

The rotation of Earth and the exchange of heat between the atmosphere and the oceans create wind and ocean currents. At the equator, trade winds blow westward over the Pacific, pushing surface water away from South America toward Australia and Indonesia. These strong trade winds, laden with moisture, bring life-giving monsoons to eastern Asia. As warm surface water moves west, cold, nutrient-rich water from deep in the ocean rises to replace it. Along the coast of Peru, this pattern creates a rich fishing ground.

Every three to five years, however, the trade winds slacken, or even reverse direction, allowing winds from the west to push warm surface water eastward toward South America. This change is called the Southern Oscillation (oscillation means swinging or swaying), and it is brought about by a shifting pattern of air pressure between the eastern and western ends of the Pacific Ocean. The warm water, lacking nutrients, kills marine life and upsets the ocean food chain. The warm, moist air that slams into the South American coast brings heavy rains and storms. At the same time, countries at the western end of the Pacific—Australia, Indonesia, and the Philippines—have unusually dry weather that sometimes causes drought and wildfires.

Another type of unusual weather that often follows an El Niño is called La Niña, which is Spanish for "the girl." El Niño and La Niña are opposite phases in the Southern Oscillation, or the back and forth cycle in the Pacific Ocean. Whereas El Niño is a warming trend, raising the water temperature as much as 10°F (5.6°C) above normal, La Niña is a cooling of the waters in the tropical Pacific, dropping the temperature of the water as much as 15°F (8°C) below normal.

Global effects of El Niño

Meteorologists believe the altered pattern of winds and ocean temperatures during an El Niño changes the high level winds, called the jet

Words to Know

Jet streams: High velocity winds that blow at upper levels in the atmosphere and help to steer major storm systems.

Monsoon: An annual shift in the direction of the prevailing wind that brings on a rainy season and affects large parts of Asia and Africa.

streams, that steer storms over North and South America. El Niños have been linked with milder winters in western Canada and the northern United States, as more severe storms are steered northward to Alaska. The jet streams altered by El Niño can also contribute to storm development over the Gulf of Mexico, which brings heavy rains to the southeastern United States. Similar rains may soak countries of South America, such as Peru and Ecuador, while droughts may affect Bolivia and parts of Central America.

El Niño also appears to affect monsoons, which are annual shifts in the prevailing winds that bring on rainy seasons. The rains of the monsoons are critical for agriculture in India, Southeast Asia, and portions of Africa. When the monsoons fail, millions of people are at risk of starvation. It appears that wind patterns associated with El Niños carry away moist air that would produce monsoon rains.

La Niña can bring cold winters to the Pacific Northwest, northern Plains states, Great Lakes states, and Canada, and warmer-than-usual winters to the southeastern states. In addition, it can bring drier-than-usual conditions to California, the Southwest, the Gulf of Mexico, and Florida, as well as drought for the South America coast and flooding for the western Pacific region.

Not all El Niños and La Niñas have equally strong effects on global climate; every El Niño and La Niña event is different, both in strength and length.

Worst El Niños of the century

According the National Oceanic and Atmospheric Administration (NOAA), 23 El Niños and 15 La Niñas took place in the twentieth century. Out of those, the four strongest occurred after 1980. Scientists are unsure if this is an indication that human activity is adversely affecting the weather or if it is simply a meaningless random clustering.

The El Niño event of 1982–83 was one of the most destructive of the twentieth century. It caused catastrophic weather patterns around the world. Devastating droughts hit Africa and Australia while torrential rains plagued Peru and Ecuador. In the United States, record snow fell in parts of the Rocky Mountains; drenching rains flooded Florida and the Gulf of Mexico's coast; and intense storms brought about floods and

Severe drought in Botswana, Africa, was the result of an El Niño weather pattern that began in 1989. *(Reproduced by permission of The Stock Market.)*

mud slides in southern California. French Polynesia in the South Pacific was struck by its first typhoon in 75 years. It is estimated this particular El Niño killed 2,000 people and caused $13 billion worth of property damage.

Less than 15 years later, another destructive El Niño pattern developed. This one, however, was much more devastating than the 1982-83 event. In fact, it was the worst in recorded history. Beginning in late 1997, heavy rain and flooding overwhelmed the Pacific coast of South America, California, and areas along the Gulf Coast. Eastern Europe and East Africa were affected, as well. Australia, Central America, Mexico, northeastern Brazil, Southeast Asia, and the southern United States were all hit hard by drought and wildfires. In the United States, mudslides and flash floods covered communities from California to Mississippi. A series of hurricanes swept through the eastern and western Pacific. Southeast Asia suffered through its worst drought in fifty years. As a result, the jungle fires used to clear lands for farming raged out of control, producing smoke that created the worst pollution crisis in world history. At least 1,000 people died from breathing problems. By the time this El Niño period ended some eight months later in 1998, the unusual weather patterns it had created had killed approximately 2,100 people and caused at least $33 billion in property damage.

[*See also* **Atmospheric pressure; Ocean; Weather; Wind**]

Embryo and embryonic development

The term embryo applies to the earliest form of life, produced when an egg (female reproductive cell) is fertilized by a sperm (male reproductive cell; semen). The fertilized egg is called a zygote. Shortly after fertilization, the zygote begins to grow and develop. It divides to form two cells, then four, then eight, and so on. As the zygote and its daughter cells divide, they start to become specialized, meaning they begin to take on characteristic structures and functions that will be needed in the adult plant or animal.

An embryo is a living organism, like a full-grown rose bush, frog, or human. It has the same needs—food, oxygen, warmth, and protection—that the adult organism has. These needs are provided for in a variety of ways by different kinds of organisms.

Words to Know

Differentiation: The process by which cells mature into specialized cell types, such as blood cells, muscle cells, brain cells, and sex cells.

Ectoderm: The outer layer or cells in the multilayered embryo.

Endoderm: The innermost wall of a multilayered embryo.

Fetus: In the higher vertebrates, the complex stage of development that follows the completion of the embryonic stage until hatching or birth.

Mesoderm: The central layer of cells in an embryo covered by three walls.

Ultrasonography: A process used to obtain "pictures" of the developing embryo using ultrasound.

Zygote: A fertilized egg.

Embryology

The study of changes that take place in the embryo is known as embryology. As one might imagine, the subject of embryology has fascinated humans since the dawn of time. Every culture has had its own theories and beliefs as to how the young of any species are created and born. The earliest formal writings on embryology can be traced to about 1416 B.C. in India. A document in Sanskrit (an ancient Indian language) describes the origin of the embryo being the union of the blood from the mother and semen from the father. Although this is not completly accurate, the document goes on to describe various stages of embryo development.

Our modern understanding of changes that take place within the embryo can be traced to the rise of the cell theory in about 1838. Scientists finally discovered the process by which sperm cells from a male and egg cells from a female combine to form a zygote. Studies by the Austrian monk Gregor Mendel (1822–1884) opened a way to explain how genetic characteristics were transmitted from one generation to the next. Finally, in 1953, the discovery of the molecular structure of DNA (deoxyribonucleic acid) by the American biologist James Watson (1928–) and the English chemist Francis Crick (1916–) provided a chemical explanation of changes that take place during fertilization and development.

Embryonic development

The term embryonic development refers to changes that take place as an embryo matures. Those changes differ from plants to animals and from species to species. The discussion that follows focuses on embryonic development in humans.

The zygote forms in one of the mother's fallopian tubes, the tubes that connect the ovaries with the uterus. It then travels to the uterus, where it becomes affixed to the uterine lining. Along the way, the zygote divides a number of times. By the time it reaches the uterus, it consists of about 100 cells and is called an embryoblast.

The exact day on which the embryoblast implants on the uterine wall varies, but is usually about the sixth day after fertilization. By the end of the first week, a protective sac, the amniotic cavity, begins to form around the embryoblast. Changes now begin to take place at a rapid rate.

During week two of embryonic development, embryonic cells have begun the process of differentiation. The identical cells formed by the early divisions of the zygote are beginning to take on the different characteristic of muscle, blood, nerve, bone, and other kinds of cells. The embryo has burrowed deep into the uterine wall and is visible as a bump on the inner uterine surface. This position permits the embryo to receive oxygen and nutrients from the mother's blood and to excrete waste products into her bloodstream.

Miscarriages are not uncommon at this stage of pregnancy. The mother's immune system may react to cells from the embryo that it classifies as "foreign" and will begin to attack those cells. The embryo may die and be expelled.

During week three the embryo grows to a length of about 0.08 inches (2 millimeters) long and has become pear-shaped with a rounded head and a tapered tail end. Three distinct types of cells can be distinguished. Ectoderm cells will form the embryo's skin; mesoderm cells its bones, muscles, and organs; and endoderm cells its digestive tract.

Blood vessels have begun to form and, by day 20, the embryo has developed its own arteries and veins. Cells begin to collect along the embryo's back in a formation known as the neural tube, a structure that will eventually develop into the brain and spinal cord.

During the fourth week, the embryo becomes C-shaped with an enlarged forebrain and a visible tail. Eye stalks and ear pits appear. Upper and lower limb buds are observable. Lung, liver, pancreatic, and gall bladder buds emerge. The umbilical cord and early facial areas also form. By the end of this week, the embryo is comprised of millions of cells and is about 0.12 to 0.16 inches (3 to 4 millimeters) long. To the naked eye, the embryo looks like a small oval.

Extensive neural (nerve) and cardiac (heart) development takes place this week. Early bone formations, that will later be the vertebrae, appear along the neural tube. Nerves, muscle, and connective tissues emerge around the primitive bone formations.

By the end of fifth week, the embryo is almost 0.5 inch (about 7 to 9 millimeters) long and has all of its internal organs. The external ears emerge, and upper limb buds extend to form paddlelike hands. The mouth, stomach, and urinary bladder are present. Nose pits and eye lenses are visible. A few days after upper limb bud extension, the lower limb buds evolve further. Much more brain development occurs at this time, and the head enlarges, causing it to bend forward and appear large compared to the body. The umbilical cord becomes more clearly defined.

During the sixth week, the trunk straightens and upper limb development continues. The neck, elbows, and wrists form. Mammary and pituitary gland buds appear. Bone, cartilage, and muscles become defined around the spinal cord and in the embryonic chest. Early in this week, tooth buds appear. These buds will become the "baby" teeth that are lost in childhood. Rib cells line up horizontally along the trunk sides, and skin

A human embryo at five to six weeks of development. *(Reproduced by permission of Photo Researchers, Inc.)*

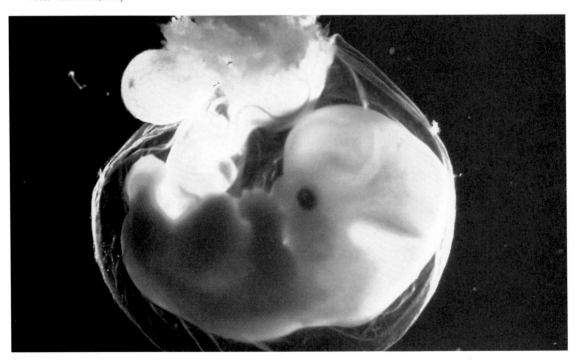

layers that will hold sweat glands develop. The regions of the brain that will become the cerebral hemispheres are very prominent at this time. The embryo appears more human by this point. It is about 0.44 to 0.56 inch (11 to 14 millimeters) long, and its heart is beating at the rate of 140 to 150 beats per minute.

During the seventh week, future fingers and thumbs are clearly visible on the hands. The torso lengthens, the tail begins to disappear, and the primitive organs continue to evolve. The heart has become divided into chambers. The cornea of the eye is also present. By the end of this week, the embryo is about 0.8 inch (20 millimeters) long and about the size of a quarter.

During the eighth week, remarkable development occurs. Nerve cells in the brain form at a rate of about 100,000 a minute. The top of the head becomes more rounded and erect. Between day 52 and day 56, the fan-shaped toes go from being webbed to separated. The fingers are entirely distinct. The eyelids close over the eyes and become fused shut until about the twenty-sixth week. External genital (sex organ) differences begin to develop. All appearances of the tail are gone. By day 56, the embryo is roughly 1 to 1.25 inches (27 to 31 millimeters) long.

Continued development

The first three months of embryonic development are known as the first trimester, that is, the first three-month period of growth. At the end of the first trimester, the embryo looks like an adult, with all major organs having been formed. It is about 3 inches (7.5 centimeters) long. Still, an embryo born during this period trimester will not survive. Additional time in the mother's womb is needed to permit further development of the organs.

At the beginning of the second trimester, the growing organism is no longer called an embryo, but a fetus. Fetal development continues through the second and third trimesters until it is ready for birth at the end of the ninth month.

Embryo diagnosis

A number of techniques have been developed to study the development of the embryo. These techniques can be used to determine the presence of problems in the growing embryo.

An ultrasound diagnosis can be performed at any time during pregnancy. Ultrasound diagnosis is a type of technology that uses high-pitched

Embryonic Transfer

Imagine a baby with two mothers! At one time, that idea may have seemed absurd. Today, the practice is common. It is accomplished by a procedure known as embryonic transfer. Embryonic transfer is carried out by removing the eggs from one female and transferring them into the body of another female. The embryos have, in effect, two mothers: the one that provided the egg necessary for fertilization and the one that provided the uterus during pregnancy.

Embryonic transfer has been widely used among animal breeders to increase the number of offspring from a valuable cow, sheep, or horse. Some endangered species have benefitted from zoo breeding programs that use embryonic transfer. In humans, embryonic transfer is sometimes used as part of a fertility program. Egg donation or the use of a surrogate uterus offers hope to infertile women who have healthy eggs but lack either normal ovaries or a normal uterus.

The technique used in embryonic transfer is typified in the procedure used with domestic animals. A prize female is stimulated with hormones (organic chemicals) to produce many eggs. These eggs are then fertilized, either through normal breeding or artificial insemination, with the sperm of a champion male. Next the embryos are flushed from the uterus with a saline (salt-water) solution. Scientists use a microscope to search for the tiny clump of cells that signify an embryo at this stage. Once found, the embryos are ready for transfer. They can also be frozen for future thawing and use, if desired. When

sounds that cannot be heard by the human ear. The sound is bounced off of the embryo and the echoes received are used to identify embryonic size. The technique is similar to the one used by submarines to locate underwater structures. By 18 weeks of pregnancy, ultrasound technology can detect structural abnormalities such as spina bifida (various defects of the spine), hydrocephaly (water on the brain), anencephaly (no brain), heart and kidney defects, and harelip (in which the upper lip is divided into two or more parts).

Chorionic villus sampling (CVS) is the most sophisticated modern technique used to assess possible inherited, genetic defects. This test is usually performed between the sixth and eighth week of embryonic development. During the test, a narrow tube is passed through the vagina or the abdomen, and a sample of the chorionic villi is removed while the

the embryos are implanted, a syringelike device delivers them into the uterus of the foster mother. If multiple embryos exist, multiple foster mothers are needed.

Breeders can typically produce six calves from one embryonic transfer. In this manner, a single prized cow can produce many calves each year. With proper training and equipment, embryonic transfer can be mastered by cattle farmers themselves.

A similar procedure is used in humans when a woman who is not able to produce eggs wishes to have a baby. Another woman is found to serve as an egg donor. The egg donor may be a close relative or may be anonymous, just as the men who donate to sperm banks are anonymous.

Several donor eggs are retrieved through a minor operation. The egg from the donor and the sperm from the male are combined in the lab in a procedure known as in vitro fertilization. The fertilized egg is then implanted in the infertile woman's uterus for a normal pregnancy and birth. Three months of hormone treatment are needed to establish the pregnancy. After that, the hormones produced normally by the woman are enough to maintain the pregnancy. Nine months later, the infertile woman gives birth to a baby to whom she bears no genetic relationship. Although much less common than in vitro fertilization, embryonic transfer offers couples a higher success rate.

physician views the baby via an ultrasound. Chorionic villi are small hair-like projections on the covering of the embryonic sac. They are rich in both embryonic and maternal blood cells. By studying these embryonic cells, genetic counselors can determine whether the baby will have any of several defects, including Down syndrome (characterized by mental retardation, short stature, and a broadened face), cystic fibrosis (which affects the digestive and respiratory systems), and the blood diseases hemophilia, sickle-cell anemia, and thalassemia. It can also show the baby's gender.

[*See also* **Fertilization**]

Where to Learn More

Books

Earth Sciences

Cox, Reg, and Neil Morris. *The Natural World*. Philadelphia, PA: Chelsea House, 2000.

Dasch, E. Julius, editor. *Earth Sciences for Students*. Four volumes. New York: Macmillan Reference, 1999.

Denecke, Edward J., Jr. *Let's Review: Earth Science*. Second edition. Hauppauge, NY: Barron's, 2001.

Engelbert, Phillis. *Dangerous Planet: The Science of Natural Disasters*. Three volumes. Farmington Hills, MI: UXL, 2001.

Gardner, Robert. *Human Evolution*. New York: Franklin Watts, 1999.

Hall, Stephen. *Exploring the Oceans*. Milwaukee, WI: Gareth Stevens, 2000.

Knapp, Brian. *Earth Science: Discovering the Secrets of the Earth*. Eight volumes. Danbury, CT: Grolier Educational, 2000.

Llewellyn, Claire. *Our Planet Earth*. New York: Scholastic Reference, 1997.

Moloney, Norah. *The Young Oxford Book of Archaeology*. New York: Oxford University Press, 1997.

Nardo, Don. *Origin of Species: Darwin's Theory of Evolution*. San Diego, CA: Lucent Books, 2001.

Silverstein, Alvin, Virginia Silverstein, and Laura Silverstein Nunn.*Weather and Climate*. Brookfield, CN: Twenty-First Century Books, 1998.

Williams, Bob, Bob Ashley, Larry Underwood, and Jack Herschbach. *Geography*. Parsippany, NJ: Dale Seymour Publications, 1997.

Life Sciences

Barrett, Paul M. *National Geographic Dinosaurs*. Washington, D.C.: National Geographic Society, 2001.

Fullick, Ann. *The Living World*. Des Plaines, IL: Heinemann Library, 1999.

Gamlin, Linda. *Eyewitness: Evolution*. New York: Dorling Kindersley, 2000.

Greenaway, Theresa. *The Plant Kingdom: A Guide to Plant Classification and Biodiversity*. Austin, TX: Raintree Steck-Vaughn, 2000.

Kidd, J. S., and Renee A Kidd. *Life Lines: The Story of the New Genetics*. New York: Facts on File, 1999.

Kinney, Karin, editor. *Our Environment*. Alexandria, VA: Time-Life Books, 2000.

Nagel, Rob. *Body by Design: From the Digestive System to the Skeleton.* Two volumes. Farmington Hills, MI: UXL., 2000.

Parker, Steve. *The Beginner's Guide to Animal Autopsy: A "Hands-in" Approach to Zoology, the World of Creatures and What's Inside Them.* Brookfield, CN: Copper Beech Books, 1997.

Pringle, Laurence. *Global Warming: The Threat of Earth's Changing Climate.* New York: SeaStar Books, 2001.

Riley, Peter. *Plant Life.* New York: Franklin Watts, 1999.

Stanley, Debbie. *Genetic Engineering: The Cloning Debate.* New York: Rosen Publishing Group, 2000.

Whyman, Kate. *The Animal Kingdom: A Guide to Vertebrate Classification and Biodiversity.* Austin, TX: Raintree Steck-Vaughn, 1999.

Physical Sciences

Allen, Jerry, and Georgiana Allen. *The Horse and the Iron Ball: A Journey Through Time, Space, and Technology.* Minneapolis, MN: Lerner Publications, 2000.

Berger, Samantha, *Light.* New York: Scholastic, 1999.

Bonnet, Bob L., and Dan Keen. *Physics.* New York: Sterling Publishing, 1999.

Clark, Stuart. *Discovering the Universe.* Milwaukee, WI: Gareth Stevens, 2000.

Fleisher, Paul, and Tim Seeley. *Matter and Energy: Basic Principles of Matter and Thermodynamics.* Minneapolis, MN: Lerner Publishing, 2001.

Gribbin, John. *Eyewitness: Time and Space.* New York: Dorling Kindersley, 2000.

Holland, Simon. *Space.* New York: Dorling Kindersley, 2001.

Kidd, J. S., and Renee A. Kidd. *Quarks and Sparks: The Story of Nuclear Power.* New York: Facts on File, 1999.

Levine, Shar, and Leslie Johnstone. *The Science of Sound and Music.* New York: Sterling Publishing, 2000

Naeye, Robert. *Signals from Space: The Chandra X-ray Observatory.* Austin, TX: Raintree Steck-Vaughn, 2001.

Newmark, Ann. *Chemistry.* New York: Dorling Kindersley, 1999.

Oxlade, Chris. *Acids and Bases.* Chicago, IL: Heinemann Library, 2001.

Vogt, Gregory L. *Deep Space Astronomy.* Brookfield, CT: Twenty-First Century Books, 1999.

Technology and Engineering Sciences

Baker, Christopher W. *Scientific Visualization: The New Eyes of Science.* Brookfield, CT: Millbrook Press, 2000.

Cobb, Allan B. *Scientifically Engineered Foods: The Debate over What's on Your Plate.* New York: Rosen Publishing Group, 2000.

Cole, Michael D. *Space Launch Disaster: When Liftoff Goes Wrong.* Springfield, NJ: Enslow, 2000.

Deedrick, Tami. *The Internet.* Austin, TX: Raintree Steck-Vaughn, 2001.

DuTemple, Leslie A. *Oil Spills.* San Diego, CA: Lucent Books, 1999.

Gaines, Ann Graham. *Satellite Communication.* Mankata, MN: Smart Apple Media, 2000.

Gardner, Robert, and Dennis Shortelle. *From Talking Drums to the Internet: An Encyclopedia of Communications Technology.* Santa Barbara, CA: ABC-Clio, 1997.

Graham, Ian S. *Radio and Television.* Austin, TX: Raintree Steck-Vaughn, 2000.

Parker, Steve. *Lasers: Now and into the Future.* Englewood Cliffs, NJ: Silver Burdett Press, 1998.

Sachs, Jessica Snyder. *The Encyclopedia of Inventions*. New York: Franklin Watts, 2001.

Wilkinson, Philip. *Building*. New York: Dorling Kindersley, 2000.

Wilson, Anthony. *Communications: How the Future Began*. New York: Larousse Kingfisher Chambers, 1999.

Periodicals

Archaeology. Published by Archaeological Institute of America, 656 Beacon Street, 4th Floor, Boston, Massachusetts 02215. Also online at www.archaeology.org.

Astronomy. Published by Kalmbach Publishing Company, 21027 Crossroads Circle, Brookfield, WI 53186. Also online at www.astronomy.com.

Discover. Published by Walt Disney Magazine, Publishing Group, 500 S. Buena Vista, Burbank, CA 91521. Also online at www.discover.com.

National Geographic. Published by National Geographic Society, 17th & M Streets, NW, Washington, DC 20036. Also online at www.nationalgeographic.com.

New Scientist. Published by New Scientist, 151 Wardour St., London, England W1F 8WE. Also online at www.newscientist. com (includes links to more than 1,600 science sites).

Popular Science. Published by Times Mirror Magazines, Inc., 2 Park Ave., New York, NY 10024. Also online at www.pop-sci.com.

Science. Published by American Association for the Advancement of Science, 1333 H Street, NW, Washington, DC 20005. Also online at www.sciencemag.org.

Science News. Published by Science Service, Inc., 1719 N Street, NW, Washington, DC 20036. Also online at www. sciencenews.org.

Scientific American. Published by Scientific American, Inc., 415 Madison Ave, New York, NY 10017. Also online at www.sciam.com.

Smithsonian. Published by Smithsonian Institution, Arts & Industries Bldg., 900 Jefferson Dr., Washington, DC 20560. Also online at www.smithsonianmag.com.

Weatherwise. Published by Heldref Publications, 1319 Eighteenth St., NW, Washington, DC 20036. Also online at www. weatherwise.org.

Web Sites

Cyber Anatomy (provides detailed information on eleven body systems and the special senses) *http://library.thinkquest.org/11965/*

The DNA Learning Center (provides in-depth information about genes for students and educators) *http://vector.cshl.org/*

Educational Hotlists at the Franklin Institute (provides extensive links and other resources on science subjects ranging from animals to wind energy) *http://sln.fi.edu/tfi/ hotlists/hotlists.html*

ENC Web Links: Science (provides an extensive list of links to sites covering subject areas under earth and space science, physical science, life science, process skills, and the history of science) *http:// www.enc.org/weblinks/science/*

ENC Web Links: Math topics (provides an extensive list of links to sites covering subject areas under topics such as advanced mathematics, algebra, geometry, data analysis and probability, applied mathematics, numbers and operations, measurement, and problem solving) *http://www. enc.org/weblinks/math/*

Encyclopaedia Britannica Discovering Dinosaurs Activity Guide *http://dinosaurs.eb. com/dinosaurs/study/*

The Exploratorium: The Museum of Science, Art, and Human Perception *http:// www.exploratorium.edu/*

ExploreMath.com (provides highly interactive math activities for students and educators) *http://www.exploremath.com/*

ExploreScience.com (provides highly interactive science activities for students and educators) *http://www.explorescience.com/*

Imagine the Universe! (provides information about the universe for students aged 14 and up) *http://imagine.gsfc.nasa.gov/*

Mad Sci Network (highly searchable site provides extensive science information in addition to a search engine and a library to find science resources on the Internet; also allows students to submit questions to scientists) *http://www.madsci.org/*

The Math Forum (provides math-related information and resources for elementary through graduate-level students) *http://forum.swarthmore.edu/*

NASA Human Spaceflight: International Space Station (NASA homepage for the space station) *http://www.spaceflight.nasa.gov/station/*

NASA's Origins Program (provides up-to-the-minute information on the scientific quest to understand life and its place in the universe) *http://origins.jpl.nasa.gov/*

National Human Genome Research Institute (provides extensive information about the Human Genome Project) *http://www.nhgri.nih.gov:80/index.html*

New Scientist Online Magazine *http://www.newscientist.com/*

The Nine Planets (provides a multimedia tour of the history, mythology, and current scientific knowledge of each of the planets and moons in our solar system) *http://seds.lpl.arizona.edu/nineplanets/nineplanets/nineplanets.html*

The Particle Adventure (provides an interactive tour of quarks, neutrinos, antimatter, extra dimensions, dark matter, accelerators, and particle detectors) *http://particleadventure.org/*

PhysLink: Physics and astronomy online education and reference *http://physlink.com/*

Savage Earth Online (online version of the PBS series exploring earthquakes, volcanoes, tsunamis, and other seismic activity) *http://www.pbs.org/wnet/savageearth/*

Science at NASA (provides breaking information on astronomy, space science, earth science, and biological and physical sciences) *http://science.msfc.nasa.gov/*

Science Learning Network (provides Internet-guided science applications as well as many middle school science links) *http://www.sln.org/*

SciTech Daily Review (provides breaking science news and links to dozens of science and technology publications; also provides links to numerous "interesting" science sites) *http://www.scitechdaily.com/*

Space.com (space news, games, entertainment, and science fiction) *http://www.space.com/index.html*

SpaceDaily.com (provides latest news about space and space travel) *http://www.spacedaily.com/*

SpaceWeather.com (science news and information about the Sun-Earth environment) *http://www.spaceweather.com/*

The Why Files (exploration of the science behind the news; funded by the National Science Foundation) *http://whyfiles.org/*

Index

Italic type indicates volume numbers; **boldface** type indicates entries and their page numbers; (ill.) indicates illustrations.

A

Abacus *1:* **1-2** 1 (ill.)
Abelson, Philip *1:* 24
Abortion *3:* 565
Abrasives *1:* **2-4,** 3 (ill.)
Absolute dating *4:* 616
Absolute zero *3:* 595-596
Abyssal plains *7:* 1411
Acceleration *1:* **4-6**
Acetylsalicylic acid *1:* **6-9,** 8 (ill.)
Acheson, Edward G. *1:* 2
Acid rain *1:* **9-14,** 10 (ill.), 12 (ill.), *6:* 1163, *8:* 1553
Acidifying agents *1:* 66
Acids and bases *1:* **14-16,** *8:* 1495
Acoustics *1:* **17-23,** 17 (ill.), 20 (ill.)
Acquired immunodeficiency syndrome. *See* **AIDS (acquired immunodeficiency syndrome)**
Acrophobia *8:* 1497
Actinides *1:* **23-26,** 24 (ill.)
Acupressure *1:* 121
Acupuncture *1:* 121
Adams, John Couch *7:* 1330
Adaptation *1:* **26-32,** 29 (ill.), 30 (ill.)
Addiction *1:* **32-37,** 35 (ill.), *3:* 478
Addison's disease *5:* 801

Adena burial mounds *7:* 1300
Adenosine triphosphate *7:* 1258
ADHD *2:* 237-238
Adhesives *1:* **37-39,** 38 (ill.)
Adiabatic demagnetization *3:* 597
ADP *7:* 1258
Adrenal glands *5:* 796 (ill.)
Adrenaline *5:* 800
Aerobic respiration *9:* 1673
Aerodynamics *1:* **39-43,** 40 (ill.)
Aerosols *1:* **43-49,** 43 (ill.)
Africa *1:* **49-54,** 50 (ill.), 53 (ill.)
Afterburners *6:* 1146
Agent Orange *1:* **54-59,** 57 (ill.)
Aging and death *1:* **59-62**
Agoraphobia *8:* 1497
Agriculture *1:* **62-65,** 63, 64 (ill.), *3:*582-590, *5:* 902-903, *9:* 1743-744, *7:* 1433 (ill.)
Agrochemicals *1:* **65-69,** 67 (ill.), 68 (ill.)
Agroecosystems *2:* 302
AI. *See* **Artificial intelligence**
AIDS (acquired immunodeficiency syndrome) *1:* **70-74,** 72 (ill.), *8:* 1583, *9:* 1737
Air flow *1:* 40 (ill.)
Air masses and fronts *1:* **80-82,** 80 (ill.)
Air pollution *8:* 1552, 1558
Aircraft *1:* **74-79,** 75 (ill.), 78 (ill.)
Airfoil *1:* 41
Airplanes. *See* **Aircraft**
Airships *1:* 75

E

1068, 1062 (ill.), 1065 (ill.), 1066 (ill.)
Human-dominated biomes *2:* 302
Humanistic psychology *8:* 1596
Humason, Milton *9:* 1655
Hurricanes *3:* 610
Hutton, James *10:* 1947
Huygens, Christiaan *6:* 1187, *9:* 1711
Hybridization *2:* 310
Hydrocarbons *7:* 1430-1431
Hydrogen *6:* **1068-1071,** 1068 (ill.)
Hydrologic cycle *6:* **1071-1075,** 1072 (ill.), 1073 (ill.)
Hydropower *1:* 113
Hydrosphere *2:* 305
Hydrothermal vents *7:* 1418, 1417 (ill.)
Hygrometer *10:* 2020
Hypertension *3:* 484
Hypertext *6:* 1128
Hypnotherapy *1:* 119
Hypotenuse *10:* 1932
Hypothalamus *2:* 342, 343
Hypothesis *9:* 1723

I

Icarus *1:* 74
Ice ages *6:* **1075-1078,** 1077 (ill.)
Icebergs *6:* **1078-1081**, 1080 (ill.), 1081 (ill.)
Idiot savants. *See* **Savants**
IgE *1:* 109
Igneous rock *9:* 1702
Ileum *4:* 656
Imaginary numbers *6:* **1081-1082**
Immune system *1:* 108, *6:* **1082-1087**
Immunization *1:* 161, *10:* 1060-1960
Immunoglobulins *1:* 159
Imprinting *2:* 272
In vitro fertilization *4:* 791
Incandescent light *6:* **1087-1090,** 1089 (ill.)
Inclined plane *6:* 1207
Indian peninsula *1:* 197
Indicator species *6:* **1090-1092,** 1091 (ill.)
Indium *1:* 126
Induction *4:* 760

Industrial minerals *6:* **1092-1097**
Industrial Revolution *1:* 28, *3:* 523, *6:* 1193, **1097-1100,** *7:* 1236, *9:* 1817
automation *2:* 242
effect on agriculture *1:* 63
food preservation *5:* 892
Infantile paralysis. *See* **Poliomyelitis**
Infants, sudden death. *See* **Sudden infant death syndrome (SIDS)**
Inflationary theory *2:* 275, 276
Influenza *4:* 672, *6:* 1084, *10:* 1978, 1979-1981
Infrared Astronomical Satellite *9:* 1808
Infrared astronomy *6:* **1100-1103,** 1102 (ill.)
Infrared telescopes *6:* 1101
Ingestion *4:* 653
Inheritance, laws of. *See* **Mendelian laws of inheritance**
Insecticides *1:* 67
Insects *6:* **1103-1106,** 1104 (ill.)
Insomnia *9:* 1747
Insulin *3:* 474, *4:* 638
Integers *1:* 180
Integral calculus *2:* 372
Integrated circuits *6:* **1106-1109,** 1108 (ill.), 1109 (ill.)
Integumentary system *6:* **1109-1112,** 1111 (ill.)
Interference *6:* **1112-1114,** 1113 (ill.)
Interferometer *6:* 1115 (ill.), 1116
Interferometry *10:* 1874, *6:* **1114-1116,** 1115 (ill.), 1116 (ill.)
Interferon *6:* 1084
Internal-combustion engines *6:* **1117-1119,** 1118 (ill.)
International Space Station *9:* 1788
International System of Units *2:* 376
International Ultraviolet Explorer *10:* 1946, *6:* **1120-1123,** 1122 (ill.)
Internet *6:* **1123-1130,** 1127 (ill.)
Interstellar matter *6:* **1130-1133,** 1132 (ill.)
Invertebrates *6:* **1133-1134,** 1134 (ill.)
Invertebrates, age of *8:* 1461
Io *6:* 1148, 1149
Iodine *6:* 1035
Ionic bonding *3:* 455
Ionization *6:* **1135-1137**
Ionization energy *6:* 1135

M

O

Oberon   *10:* 1954

Obesity   *4:* 716

Obsession   *7:* **1405-1407**

Obsessive-compulsive disorder   *7:* 1405

Obsessive-compulsive personality disorder   *7:* 1406

Occluded fronts   *1:* 82

Ocean   *7:* **1407-1411,** 1407 (ill.)

Ocean currents   *3:* 604-605

Ocean ridges   *7:* 1410 (ill.)

Ocean zones   *7:* **1414-1418**

Oceanic archaeology.   *See* **Nautical archaeology**

Oceanic ridges   *7:* 1409

Oceanography   *7:* **1411-1414,** 1412 (ill.), 1413 (ill.)

Octopus   *7:* 1289

Oersted, Hans Christian   *1:* 124, *4:* 760, 766, *6:* 1212

Offshore drilling   *7:* 1421

Ohio River   *7:* 1355

Ohm (O)   *4:* 738

Ohm, Georg Simon   *4:* 738

Ohm's law   *4:* 740

Oil drilling   *7:* **1418-1422,** 1420 (ill.)

Oil pollution   *7:* 1424

Oil spills   *7:* **1422-1426,** 1422 (ill.), 1425 (ill.)

Oils   *6:* 1191

Olduvai Gorge   *6:* 1058

Olfaction.   *See* **Smell**

On the Origin of Species by Means of Natural Selection   *6:* 1054

On the Structure of the Human Body   *1:* 139

O'Neill, J. A.   *6:* 1211

Onnes, Heike Kamerlingh   *10:* 1850

Oort cloud   *3:* 530

Oort, Jan   *8:* 1637

Open clusters   *9:* 1808

Open ocean biome   *2:* 299

Operant conditioning   *9:* 1658

Ophediophobia   *8:* 1497

Opiates   *1:* 32

Opium   *1:* 32, 33

Orangutans   *8:* 1572, 1574 (ill.)

Orbit   *7:* **1426-1428**

Organ of Corti   *4:* 695

Organic chemistry   *7:* **1428-1431**

Organic families   *7:* 1430

Organic farming   *7:* **1431-1434,** 1433 (ill.)

Origin of life   *4:* 702

Origins of algebra   *1:* 97

Orizaba, Pico de   *7:* 1359

Orthopedics   *7:* **1434-1436**

Oscilloscopes   *10:* 1962

Osmosis   *4:* 652, *7:* **1436-1439,** 1437 (ill.)

Osmotic pressure   *7:* 1436

Osteoarthritis   *1:* 181

Osteoporosis   *9:* 1742

Otitis media   *4:* 697

Otosclerosis   *4:* 697

Ovaries   *5:* 800

Oxbow lakes   *6:* 1160

Oxidation-reduction reactions   *7:* **1439-1442,** *9:* 1648

Oxone layer   *7:* 1452 (ill.)

Oxygen family   *7:* **1442-1450,** 1448 (ill.)

Ozone   *7:* **1450-1455,** 1452 (ill.)

Ozone depletion   *1:* 48, *8:* 1555

Ozone layer   *7:* 1451

P

Packet switching   *6:* 1124

Pain   *7:* 1336

Paleoecology   *8:* **1457-1459,** 1458 (ill.)

Paleontology   *8:* **1459-1462,** 1461 (ill.)

Paleozoic era   *5:* 990, *8:* 1461

Paleozoology   *8:* 1459

Panama Canal   *6:* 1194

Pancreas   *4:* 655, *5:* 798

Pangaea   *8:* 1534, 1536 (ill.)

Pap test   *5:* 1020

Papanicolaou, George   *5:* 1020

Paper   *8:* **1462-1467,** 1464 (ill.), 1465 (ill.), 1466 (ill.)

Papyrus   *8:* 1463

Paracelsus, Philippus Aureolus   *1:* 84

Parasites   *8:* **1467-1475,** 1471 (ill.), 1472 (ill.), 1474 (ill.)

Parasitology   *8:* 1469

Parathyroid glands   *5:* 798

Paré, Ambroise   *8:* 1580, *10:* 1855

Parkinson's disease   *1:* 62

Parsons, Charles A.   *9:* 1820

Particle accelerators   *8:* **1475-1482,**

W

X

Y